Em

MW00800999

Emus Keeping, Care, Housing, Interaction, Diet and Health
by

Roger Rodendale

Table of Contents

Introduction

Emus have been raised as pets for several years, mostly because of their lean meat, and farming for this meat became popular after the 'Emu War'. We will discuss the Emu war in greater detail in the following chapters.

This bird is native to Australia and is the largest bird that originates in this region. While farming these birds is still a very lucrative commercial venture, many Emu owners have come to realize that these birds also make wonderful pets because of their sweet and friendly nature.

Of course, you need to be extremely cautious while raising Emus, as they are really large birds that can become unruly and dangerous when not raised to be tame. There are a few thumb rules with Emus such as opting for younger birds if this is the first time you are dealing with this bird. You will learn about several such rules and tips in this book. All these ideas have come from experienced Emu owners.

There are several things about the Emu that make them the most adorable pets to have at home. They are wonderfully friendly and can even be very playful around the people that they have bonded with. The gait of these birds and the "goofy expression that they carry makes them a lot more fun to be around.

When they are larger, there are several restrictions with respect to the space and the area that you can raise these birds in. However, if you raise

Emus as babies, you will see that they are just as great as any other household pet that climbs up into your lap, hides in small spaces in your home and just keeps you entertained all day.

But, it is very important for you to remember that an Emu is not like another pet that you can bring out with you and keep at your home. These birds require a lot of planning. Most people who have had Emus before would equate it to bringing home a horse. Housing the bird is one of the biggest concerns as they are extremely large and need a lot of exercise in order to stay fit and healthy. It is impossible to have an Emu at home if you do not have space. You wouldn't cram a horse into an apartment, would you?

This book is the best guide for anyone who is setting out on their journey with their Emus. It will provide you with all the information that you require from sourcing your bird, housing them and even providing them with proper nutrition and care. The information that you will find in this book has been tested by Emu owners, therefore all the tips are practical and easy.

In totality, this book gives a complete insight into the world of an Emu parent, to understand what goes into taking care of them.

Chapter 1: Meet the Emus

Emus are birds that cannot fly. They are native to Australia and belong to a certain group of birds that are popularly known as Ratites. These birds can be found all over Australia, except in the crowded cities, the dense forests and the deserts. You will mostly see an Emu in areas that are primarily grasslands or Savannahs.

Today, Emus are popular globally for their commercial value. And, besides that, these birds can make wonderful companions when reared properly and trained to live among human beings.

1. Physical description

It is very easy to identify an Emu thanks to its unique build and rather recognizable head shape. But, it is natural for novices to get severely confused between an Ostrich and an Emu. This chapter will help you identify the Emu bird and also understand the standards that are used to identify a healthy Emu specimen.

The first thing you need to know about Emus is that they are large birds. At the time that they hatch they are about 10 inches tall. They grow quite fast and can be about 54 inches in height just at 6 months of age. Adult Emus can grow up to 6 feet in height! The shoulder width goes up to 4 feet.

A mature Emu, who is approximately two years old, will weigh anything between 65 to 100 pounds. The heaviest recorded Emu is about 130 pounds in weight!

The Emu has a flat sternum that almost looks like a raft. There is no keel that the wing is normally attached to. This is seen in all birds that can fly and even in some birds that are not capable of flying.

However, Emus do have wings. These are tiny vestigial wings. The most characteristic features of an Emu are the long legs and the long neck. The pelvic limb of these birds have a very typical musculature that allows them to run at very high speeds quite conveniently.

The feet of an Emu has only three toes. They also have fewer bones and foot muscles associated with it. These are the only birds that have a muscle called the gastrocnemius. This is what we humans commonly call the Calf Muscles. The mass of the pelvic muscles of an Emu is equivalent to the mass of the wing muscles of a bird that can fly. What this means is that the contribution of these muscles to the total body weight of the bird is more or less the same.

The feathers of these birds are usually between gray brown to fully brown. The plumage consists of soft feathers. Because of this, the bird has a very shaggy appearance. The feathers of the Emu have a very unique feature. From a single shaft, two feathers emerge. The shaft is black in color as are the tips of these feathers. The inner plumage is very loosely packed, providing insulation to the bird as needed. All the solar radiations are absorbed by the black tips and the heat does not flow into the skin thanks to the coat. This allows the Emus to flourish even in very harsh heat. As a result, they are active through the day, despite extreme heat.

The neck of the Emu is usually pale blue in color. This region is very sparse in feathers, making it possible for you to see the color of the skin quite easily. There are a few small feathers that you can see running down the middle of the head, down to the neck, making it seem almost like the bird has a Mohawk!

When the days get very hot, Emus adopt a behavior very similar to dogs. They pant and the lungs work like coolers that work on the principle of evaporation. A drop in the carbon dioxide levels is not noticed thanks to a certain mechanism known as Alkalosis. When the birds need to breathe in the normal temperatures or in colder conditions, they make use of their nasal passage that has several levels.

As the cool air is drawn in through the nasal passage, it gathers heat as it reaches the lungs. When the bird breathes out, the moisture condenses back and it is absorbed for use in the body.

There are several adaptive features that you will notice in the Emu. Since they primarily live in grasslands, they feed themselves by grazing. For this, their beaks have adapted into shorter ones to make it easier for the bird to pick the grass.

Like any other animal or bird species that lives in dry and hot conditions, the Emu does not require water consumption often. However, when they do drink water, they drink in large quantities and use the water as required.

The eyes of the Emu are also indicative of the kind of habitat that these birds are usually found in. Now, the eyes have a protective membrane called the nictitating membrane. This is a translucent layer that almost serves like a secondary eyelid for the bird. The only difference is that this eyelid moves horizontally from the inside to the outer edge of the eye, almost like a curtain!

This membrane plays the role of a visor that protects the eyes from any dust or dirt that is commonly seen in the arid regions that these birds live in.

You also need to remember that these birds are not sexually dimorphic. You cannot tell the difference between the male and the female unless you are an expert. In some cases, the penis of the male bird may become visible when he is urinating or defecating.

It is easy however, to recognize an Emu in heat as they have a pouch in the tracheal area that becomes prominent when the breeding season begins.

When you commit to an Emu, remind yourself that you are bringing home the second largest bird in the world. You really ought to prepare yourself well for that.

Unlike the other birds, Emus do not have any waterproofing on their feathers. In fact, they are considered to be a rather ugly sight when they are wet. They look extremely messy and also smell like a dog that is drenched.

These birds have a neck sac that is inflatable. It is like a pouch for the throat. This pouch is also a part of their windpipe that is mostly used to communicate. This pouch is almost 30 cm long. The sac has a very thin wall and can be inflated to make loud noises. After inflating this sac, these birds are able to make grunting sounds and booming noises too. The drumming sound is exclusive to the females. This is a distinguishing factor between the male and female birds. You will hear these sounds during the breeding season quite clearly. They are so loud that they can even be heard from as far as two kilometers away.

Emus are among the most unique birds in their appearance, the sounds that they make and also their adaptive features.

2. Distribution of Emus

These birds are native to Australia and were commonly seen on the Eastern Coast of the continent. Now, these birds are more predominant in the interior regions of the continent. The development of agriculture and the water stock available to the birds is responsible for this transition.

Emus are found in various types of habitats in Australia. They are seen near the coast as well as inland. The most common habitat, of course is

8

the savannah woodland or the sclerophyll forest. In the districts that have large human populations, Emus are not normally seen. In addition to that, any area that has less than 600mm of rainfall annually does not have Emu populations.

These birds will travel in pairs. Of course, they also form flocks that are quite large in number. The main objective of these pairs and flocks is to find a common food source and move towards it.

These birds can travel for several kilometers in search of food and in the Western part of Australia, it has been noticed that these birds have a certain seasonal pattern of migration. They tend to head North during the summers and South during the winters. On the East coast, however, the pattern is not really uniform and it is quite common to see them take random routes and paths. It almost seems like the birds in these regions are wandering without any direction that is determined by food or the season.

Initially, these birds were found all over the North coast of New South Wales. Now, these populations are restricted to the area between Red Rock and Evans head and the Bungawalbin region on the West. There have also been some records of Emu populations in the area around Port Stephens. The Emus in the NSW North coast and the Port Stephens area were also listed as a Threatened Species under the Local Government. These populations were threatened by hunting.

The main thing that Emus require for survival is water. Even the population explosion of these birds can be attributed to the water holes created by the English settlers. Ironically, it was these settlements that led to their rapid decline.

3. History

a. The Emu war
Emu birds have been living in the continent of Australia for several years. In fact, it is also believed that the ancestors of these birds lived alongside the mighty Dinosaurs. Their ancestors were called the Dromornithids. However, these birds came into light only in the 19th century. This discovery of the species led to proper description and understanding of the bird but the negative impact was that two entire species got wiped out due to hunting.

In fact, in the year 1932, a major event in the history of these birds, called the Emu War, began. The summer in this year was very hot and the birds were forced to look for food and water outside their habitat. This made them go on quite a rampage that became a hassle to several farmers in these areas.

They began to put a lot of pressure on the Australian government to get rid of these giant birds that were ruining their crops. So, the Australian government sent the Royal Australian Artillery after these birds. This operation was led by Major Meredith. The soldiers were armed with machine guns and had to fire close to 10,000 rounds on the birds. The number of birds on rampage, however, was 20,000. This led to the Emu war in which, fortunately, the Emus emerged victorious.

It was noted that these birds were very adept in camouflage. They also had better strategic retreat skills in comparison to the soldiers who were sent after them. They would disperse into little groups as soon as any bullet was fired at them.

The war had to be withdrawn in less than a week as it seemed quite aimless. The Defence Minister decided to call the war off. After one week of war only 12 birds had been killed. The soldiers and onlookers were surprised at the hardiness of the bird. They were able to suffer major injuries and continue running. Major Meredith said that an army with the bullet carrying capacity of Emus would become invincible. They would even be able to stand machine gun fires. He famously compared these birds to the Zulus.

The structure of these birds aided them to run fast and even dodge several bullets. Following this dark phase, the Emu actually became an important Australian symbol. They appeared along with the Kangaroo on the Coat of Arms. This represents a steadily growing Australian continent because, surprisingly, both animals are unable to walk backwards! These birds have also been seen on stamps since the Emu War. There are close to 600 places in Australia named after the Emus. Several products and companies were also named after the bird. The most popular product was the Emu beer that was crafted by Swan brewery.

Of course, the bird is a rather important commodity today with great importance given to the agricultural value of these low maintenance birds.

b. Emu description and studies
The first ever Emus were studied in the Western coast of Australia. When European explorers reached Australia in the year 1969 during an expedition that was led by William de Vlamingh, this bird was first noticed and recorded. This Dutch expedition had set out to look for a missing ship that had been lost at sea about two years before.

On the Eastern coast of Australia, Emus were discovered almost ten years later when European travelers settled in these areas. When the Emu was first seen, it was noted down as the New Holland cassowary. A book named Botany Bay was published in the year 1789 by Arthur Philip, which had a detailed description of the Emu.

The first thing that he noted down was that this bird was markedly different from any other birds that they knew of. The Emu was undoubtedly a large bird. But, what was special about the bird was that it had the ability to stand tall on its legs and run. The bird also had a rather peculiarly long neck.

The total height of the first Emu that was spotted was 7ft and 2 inches. The bill was very similar to the cassowary. The difference was that the bird had a horn or a helmet like appendage on the head. The bird was very different from anything they had seen before. Except for the throat and the front of the neck, the head was covered with feathers. Of course, this plumage was sparse, exposing the skin of the bird. In the case of the Cassowary, the head was similar to the Turkey and was carunculated and bare.

The typical curl or bend in the end of the feathers were intriguing to these explorers. They described these short feathers as "useless" for flight. Usually, the flight feathers of birds are different from the feathers on the body. This was not true in the case of the Emu.

Normally birds had long spines that extended into the wings, but this was not seen in the Emu. The legs were the only feature that stood out, being stout and sturdy. This was similar to the Galeated Cassowary.

The Emu was given this name by an ornithologist named John Latham in the year 1790. The name was based on a specimen that was found around modern day Sydney. Back then, this area was called New Holland.

Latham and Philip collaborated on the book and provided many descriptions of this bird. This book contained descriptions and names of many other Australian birds as well. The taxonomical name given to the Emu then was Dromaius.novaehollandae

This was the Greek word for racer. Novahollandae meant, "New Holland". So, the bird was basically named the New Holland Racer.

French ornithologist provided two generic names to the Emu in his descriptions that were written in the year 1816. These were *Dromaius and Dromicelius.*

This lead to a lot of confusion and debate that is going on till this day. The generic name *Dromaius* is used commonly and the other name is considered to be an alternative.

It is uncertain where the name "Emu" came from. It is believed that the name was given to the bird by Portuguese explorers. This is a derivation of the Arabic word for "big bird". When these explorers described the bird related to the cassowary, they named it the Emu. The name was normally used to describe cranes and other large birds like the ostrich. Other names used for the Emu by the aborigines in the Sydney basin were murawung and birabayin.

c. Export of the Emu

Emus were taken to America in the 1980's. Since then, Emu farming picked up tremendously in this area. Of course, several changes were made over the years to accommodate the demands and requirements of the industry.

Initially, private collectors purchased these birds because they were novel. Coincidentally, land prices increased at that time. As a result, ranching and small scale farming became extremely difficult for most of them to manage. That is when Emu farming came as a profitable idea to many of these farm owners.

The bird was a factor of great appeal because of its potential as a great source of meat. These birds seemed easy to maintain, as the overheads were not too high. They also needed less land in comparison to the ranches. In addition to that, these birds were mostly silent and docile.

This industry picked up momentum and several farms integrated Emus into their area. They began to keep breeding pairs, hatching chicks and rearing them and even incubating the eggs. Some of them were able to market the birds successfully as well.

The industry became more commercial after the products derived from these birds, such as the oil, began to gain popularity. This industry was also promoted by many as the new age agricultural business. Farm shows and fairs began to feature the Emu. Initially, the industry grew because of the work of these famers.

As expected, the demand for the bird increased. With that, the price of these birds increased. Emu farming began to get a lot of support and initiatives were taken to help Emu farmers communicate better. The American Emu Association was formed with 50 members back then in

1989. It soon rose to a strong membership of 6000 individuals by 1994. In the next year there were affiliations from 35 states.

In one year starting from the year 1989, the price of this bird doubled. By 1993, the demand was tenfold. Thanks to imports from Europe, the supple adequately met the demand. Naturally, the prices also dropped in the year 1995 and became more realistic. With a decrease in the prices of these birds, several individuals were highly disappointed. At the same time, those who were into Emu farming began to feel relieved as the birds became affordable. It was difficult for them to produce any end products when the live bird was that expensive.

Until the prices became affordable, theft of Emus was a big problem. The thieves used to derive profits even from birds that were defective. But, not after the price drop. The only ill effect of this period was that there were several defective birds that were released on to the market. This resulted in birds that were sub-standard. This lead to a species change or improvement as is noticed with all farm animals and birds.

Despite the constant fluctuations in the price, the Emu was seen as a farm animal that was quite viable. This bird was easier to raise, it was suited to most ecological set ups and was also quite productive.

During this time, Emu products continued to be liked by the public. The market grew consistently in North America as well as Australia. This lead to other world markets such as India that picked up Emu farming instantly. The former two countries remain in the forefront of development when it comes to the Emu industry.

Today, the American Emu Association is considered an alternative industry of agriculture. It is mostly dominated by farmers who work on a small scale. These individuals are dedicated to providing humane conditions for the Emus. These birds are given proper nutrition and care to ensure that they grow into healthy specimens.

These birds are mostly raised for the low fat meat that they produce. This is considered to be the best alternative to beef. Emu leather that was once very popular is not objectionable and has been banned by several organizations.

d. Taxonomy
For a long time the Emus were classified under the family Casuradiidae because of the cassowaries that these birds so closely resembled. These birds belonged to an order of the Ratites called the Struthiioniformes. In the year 2014, quite recently another alternative to this classification was

provided based on the mitochondrial DNA of these birds. This allows the Casauriidae to be split into a separate order which is the Casuariformes. That leaves on the Cassowaries in the Casuariidae family. The Emus became their own family, which is called the Dromaiidae.

During the times of the European settlement, the birds were classified into two separate species of *Dromaius*. Another species was recognized based on the studies conducted on the fossils of these birds.

Kangaroo Island and the Kind Island consisted of dwarf Emus or the *Dromaius baudinianus* and the *Dromaius minor*. Both these dwarf Emu species became extinct after the arrival of the European settler.

There was another sub species of the Emu that was known as the Tasmanian Emu. This bird was classified as the *Dromaius novohollandiae diemensis.* This bird became extinct around the year 1865. The mainland species remained after the extinction of these subspecies.

Emu populations in the wild fluctuated quite drastically with each decade. The populations were mainly dependent upon the rainfall in their region of inhabitation.

In the year 2009, the number of the Emus was estimated to be about 630,000 to 725,000 specimens. They were then introduced to a region off Tasmania called the Maria Island. In Southern Australia, these birds were introduced to the Kangaroo Island in the beginning of the 20th century. The Emu populations of the Maria Island were not able to flourish beyond the mid-1990s and became extinct by then. Several attempts have been made to restore these populations with the primary objective being an increase in species similar to the Tasmanian Emu. On the other hand, the birds introduced in the Kangaroo Islands were able to develop into a breeding population quite easily.

In the year 1912, three species of the Emus were recognized by Australian Ornithologist, Gregory Matthews. They were classified as the *D.n.novohollandiae, D.n.woodwardi, D.n. Rothschildi.* These three species have been heavily debated ever since their description was mentioned.

In the 'Handbook of the Birds of the World', the existence of the last two species mentioned by Matthews have been deemed invalid. The argument remains that the plumage has a few natural variations and that the nomadic nature of these birds has led to the variations.

It is largely believed that these birds have just one race in Australia. The study of the DNA of the King Island populations of the Emus show that these birds are very closely related to the mainland species. So, instead of classifying them as a separate species, it is a better idea to classify them as a sub species. Since the discovery and understanding of the Emu is relatively recent, these debates continue to occur.

e. Humans and Emus

For the European settlers and the Australian aborigines, Emus were the most important source of food. These birds are very inquisitive by nature and would easily approach people if they saw any unexpected movement of the limbs or clothing.

When in the wild, these birds tend to follow people around quite willingly. The aborigines had a very unique technique of catching these birds. They would normally spear them when they were drinking at the water holes. They were even lured to nets by imitating the calls. These birds were easy to attract and would be drawn to things like a ball of feathers or even rags.

A plant called the pitchuri thornapple was grown around a water hole and would contaminate the water. When the birds drank this water, they would get disoriented and would become very easy to catch.

The hunters even used the skin of the bird as a disguise and lured the birds using one of the methods above. The aborigines were very protective about the Emus, however. They only hunted the birds out of necessity. If the bird were killed for sport, these aborigines frowned upon them. They used every part of the carcass fully. The fat was used to make the popular Emu oil, the bones were used to make tools and the feathers were used as adornment. Even the tendons were used as a substitute to strings.

For the European settlers, the fat obtained from the Ems became a source of fuel to light lamps. These settlers also wanted to keep the birds out of their farms and, hence, made several fences and even tried to kill the birds that invaded their space.

Economic value of Emus

Of course, the Emu is the best source of food in most parts of the world. The fat obtained from these birds is medicinal in nature and is used by the aborigines to anoint their skin. It also works as a lubricant for their tools and utensils. When mixed with ochre it helps the aborigines make paint for their body and also for other adornment.

Today, these birds are extensively farmed for leather, oil and meat. The practice of commercial farming of these birds was started in the Western part of Australia during the 1970s. This is when the birds bred in captivity contributed to all the commercial products.

On a large scale, these birds are also farmed in North America. In the USA alone, you will find close to 1 million birds. Peru and China are among other countries where Emus thrive. These birds are usually given a lot of grains and then provided supplementation through grazing.

In the year 2012, Emu farming was promoted in India quite heavily. However, the Salem district farmers were advised against investing in these birds. It was believed, at that time, that more time was needed to investigate the viability of this business in India.

It was reported that several ranchers had quit the Emu business in the United States by 2013 because Emu owners had declined in numbers quite drastically.

Emu meat is considered to be extremely nutritious. It is low fat meat that is as good as other forms of lean meat. The meat is classified as red meat by the USDA. This is because the meat is red in color and has a pH value that is quite similar to beef.

The fat rendered from the Emu is used for dietary supplements, cosmetics and other therapeutic fats. The adipose tissue of the Emu is heated to make a clear oil. It is mostly made of oleic acid, palmitic acid and linolenic acid. Emu oil is also quite rich in antioxidants making it a popular product.

There is also enough evidence to suggest that this oil is also anti-inflammatory in nature. There are no extensive tests to prove this beyond doubt. In addition to that, the USDA considers Emu oil a as a drug that has been unapproved.

In any case, the oil has provided significant relief from joint pains, even more than fish oils and olive oil. It also improves the healing abilities of wounds. However, there is no understanding of why and how this oil works. A study conducted in the year 2008 also showed that Emu oil is far more effective than Ostrich oil.

Emu leather has a very typical texture that is caused by a raise in the skin around the follicles of the feathers. Their feathers are a part of decorative crafts. The eggs are also engraved to create portraits and other beautiful images.

Cultural significance of Emus

Aboriginal mythology has a special place for the Emus. There are several myths like that of the Yuwaalaraay and other people of the New South Wales region. The most popular myth of all is that the sun came into being when an Emu egg was tossed into the sky.

According to one story from the Western region of Australia, there was a man who lost his limbs after a small bird threw a boomerang at him when he annoyed it. This man then transformed into the Emu which is, incidentally, a flightless bird.

It is believed that the famous Kudraitcha man from the Central part of Australia wears footwear that is made from the feathers of the Emus. He does this to conceal his foot prints. There are several language groups of the Aborigines who claim that the dust lanes of the Milky Way galaxy actually represent an Emu. There are various rock engravings in Australia that depict Emus. Many dance forms of the aborigines also mimic these birds.

The Emu is considered an emblem of the Australian fauna. It is the unofficial national bird. It is seen on the coat of arms and is also seen on the 50 cent coin. There have been several postage stamps including the 100th anniversary pre-federation issue of the NSW pots. It is also seen on a special edition blue 2 pence coin. In the year 1994 a $1.34 stamp was out in the market with an Emu on it. The Australian Light Horse also has hats that are decorated with the feathers of the Emu.

The Emu has become part of several shows including a puppet act by Rod Hull. His show revolved around an Emu that had gone wayward. The bird has also been seen on several shows on the small screen.

Undoubtedly, human beings and the Emu share a wonderful history together. There is no doubt that these birds have become great companions over the years, thanks to their keen interest in the ways of people and their environment.

Chapter 2: Housing the Emu

Before you even consider bringing an Emu home, you need to make sure that you are fully aware of the housing requirements of this massive bird. That will help you understand whether you will be able to provide for your pet or not.

To begin with, Emus need a lot of space to thrive well. If not, they have a lot of issues related to inactivity. These issues can range from digestive disorders to neurological ones. So, make sure that you have at least ¼ acre of space to begin with if you are planning to bring Emus home.

1. The enclosure design

With an Emu, you need to understand that the bird is not only large in size but also has legs that are extremely strong. So, any enclosure that you make must be able to handle the strong physique of the bird.

The enclosure that you make should be strong but should also be able to resist any collision that these birds are likely to have. Emus will walk straight into walls or will just hurl themselves at walls from time to time. The material used should also be flexible enough to prevent any injuries to the bird.

If you are using anything synthetic or concrete, it should have a non-slip surface to take care of the bird.

a. Design principles

When you create an enclosure of the Emu, keep the following in mind:

The design should be very similar to the natural habitat of the bird. This means that there should be several furnishings within the enclosure, including an open planted enclosure. Have lots of low shrubs, grass and running area for your birds.

The aggression between Emus should be reduced by creating physical and visible barriers between the birds.
You need to have the substrate and the floor specifically designed and maintained to make sure that they are not slippery. This reduces chances of falls and injuries or diseases.

You must provide the birds with ample shelter from possible extremities in the weather. You need to make sure that they have protection and shade as required.

b. Fencing requirements

In order to protect your Emus, it is very important to invest in good quality fencing. Outdoor fencing should consists of wire mesh or any other tensile wire along with tensioners and droppers. Using barbed wire is not an option as the birds may hurt themselves.

Whatever material you choose for the fencing, make sure that it is free from any obstacles that may lead to the neck and the legs of Emu getting caught. The mesh size should be small enough to prevent any entangling. You will need fencing that measures 50X50cms for an adult Emu.

The fences that you install should be easily visible to the bird. This includes any angle on the fence too. This will help prevent any chance of collisions on the fence accidentally. In order to reduce the risk of injury, you need to make sure that the stays, the straining wires and the supports are placed outside the enclosure.

If you are using an internal frame, the minimum height is about 1.5m for an adult bird. If you have to fence baby Emus, you need to make sure that that there is a kicking board that is at least 30cm thick, at the base of the fence. This prevents their feet from getting caught.

You also need to make sure that the fence is checked regularly to keep them in good condition for the birds. The enclosures that you use should reduce the chance of any predator attacking the birds. You also need to keep predators and pests at bay with these fences. You can use any type of rodent proofing along with a fox proof fence in order to keep your birds safe.

In case there is a fence around your farm, building or home that is the outer boundary of the enclosure of your Emus, you need to make sure that you add additional barriers to keep the birds safe from any disturbance from the outside.

If you notice that some of your birds are aggressive, you have to also make an escape route for yourself or for anyone who is the keeper on your Emu farm. You cannot manage this with chicks in the same enclosure.

If the source of agitation for your Emu is being exposed to people, then you will have to arrange for double fencing or any other means of keeping the viewing area separate from the actual housing area.

c. Designing the holding area

When constructing the holding area of your Emu, you need to make sure that:

The birds can stretch, turn around and stand up.

The length of the holding area is at least three times the length of the bird.

The breath of the area is one and a half times the length of the bird.

The fencing area is Emu proof.

There are no blind spots for the entry and exit of the keeper to prevent any attack.

d. Spatial considerations

There are some laws such as the Exhibited Animal Protection Act that laid certain guidelines on the spatial requirements for Emu birds when kept as pets:

The bird should have the freedom to move vertically and horizontally.

If you have an enclosure that consists of birds of other species, you need to ensure that there are no conflicts between the Emus and these other species.

The space should be able to provide enough exercise for the bird. This leads to behavior enrichment.

These birds should have the right facilities required for social interactions as well as breeding.

For an adult Emu, the minimum space required is 200 sq. meters per bird. You need to add 100 sq. meters for every bird that you add. It is recommended that you house these birds as pairs, individuals or as trios. In case of trios you need to have two females and one male, and never the other way around. You can even house groups of Emus as long as there are equal numbers of birds of both genders. You also need to make sure that there is enough space to house large groups of Emus.

e. How to position and protect enclosures

It is best to have enclosures that face the north. This allows the warmth to be trapped within the space. Cold south-western winds are avoided when you place the enclosures towards the north. This also protects the birds from the westerly rays of the sun.

According to the Code of Emu Management and Farming laid down by the Australian government, it is the duty of the owners to make sure that the Emus do not face any harsh weather conditions. Whether you have the birds in a yard or a ranch, you need to make sure that your birds get enough protection and shade.

Enclosures must always be closed on three sides. You also need to make sure that the birds are in an area where you will be able to keep an eye on them. It is good to place a shelter in front of the enclosure of your Emu as well.

These enclosures do not require any sort of temperature management. Emus are able to survive in a wide range of temperatures because they are endothermic. However, you can help them regulate their body temperatures by installing ponds in the enclosures.

This will help the birds stay cool on hot days. Planting a lot of trees and shrubs is a must when you plan to bring home an Emu as a pet. The birds need to have the option of hiding under these trees in case the sunlight gets too harsh for them to handle. You will definitely not have to invest in any additional air conditioning facilities as far as the Emus as concerned.

f. What substrate to use?
Usually grass and dirt is used as the substrate in an Emu enclosure. The gravel is also used along the fence to protect the edge of the enclosure. This prevents any wearing out of this area. Emus tend to walk around the fence line and will ruin the ground.

Grass or dirt is preferred as it is also very easy to maintain. All you need to do is rake it regularly to keep it in top condition. Gravel only needs some hose cleaning. The only issue with gravel is that all the feces and the dirt will accumulate below the substrate and will harbor several diseases. This surface is also harder for the birds to walk on. Leaf litter is a great option as it also helps the birds when they are nesting, as this is their most preferred material.

Several enclosures have switched from grass to dirt substrate. This is because all the trampling when the birds run or walk can spoil the substrate.

However, grass is more aesthetic. If you want to have portions of grass in your Emu enclosure, you should fence it off to prevent the birds from accessing it every time. This makes it a lot easier to maintain.

You should sow your grass seeds only in a fenced area. The Emus should be allowed to access this area after it has grown fully. Then you can fence off another area and sow a new batch of grass seeds. This makes fresh grass available to the birds at all times.

When you have well maintained grass, the enclosure will look lush and quite impressive. Some enclosures will also have mixed substrates. This works on areas that are large enough for the birds to wander around.

That way your Emus will have access to grass, mud, gravel and even dirt. You can choose the substrate based on the space that you have, the number of birds you plan to house and of course, the costs involved in maintaining this area.

Remember, the substrate is the most important part of the enclosure as it determines the hygiene of the facility.

These birds will choose from the vegetation available to make their nests and to also create a sleeping area. These nests will have a lining of a thin mattress of grass. They also use trampled leaves or vegetation.

The nests are built around a bush or under a tree so that it is well protected. They even look for alternatives like a mound of rocks or fallen branches. In some cases, the eggs are laid without any nest. These eggs are surrounded by protective material like bark, feathers, dry leaves, twigs and sticks.

When your birds are ready to breed, you may have to additionally provide them with hay. They usually pick this out of the hay that is fed to them.

g. Enclosure accessories and furnishings
It is possible to include a whole range of furnishings in the Emu enclosure. Here are a few ideas for your Emu enclosure:

Rocks: Different sized rocks that are available in a host of shapes can be used in the cages. Place these rocks in mounds for the Emus to use to protect themselves and their nests.

Long grass: As mentioned above, long grass can play a very important aesthetic role in the enclosures. It gives the enclosure a naturalistic appeal. The grass is a good nesting material and also serves as food for the Emus.

Bracken fern: Bracken fern makes the enclosure look even more naturalistic. The birds really enjoy bracken fern as a food item. The birds love to forage through this fern when it is placed at regular intervals around the farm.

Logs: Adding logs can also serve as a great recreational furnishing for your Emus. They will also use these rocks as spots to place their nests or lay eggs.

Ponds: You must try and include a small pond in your Emu enclosure. Not only does this serve as a great way for the birds to cool off, it is also necessary for exercises and physical activities.

As discussed in the previous chapter, ponds or water bodies became the main reason for Emu populations to thrive in Australia. These birds love to wallow in water and are also great swimmers.

The pond in your Emu enclosure should be made of any material that is suitable for your birds and does not cause any damage. The most important thing is that your bird should be able to get enough grip on the floor of the pond.

The access into and out of the pond must be easy for the Emus. The footing in the access point must be completely secure. It is recommended that the depth of the pond should be between 200mm to 1 meter.

The quality of the water must be maintained at all times. If the water does not seem pleasant, your Emu may not even go close to the pond. It is also true that a dirty pond is a harboring ground for several microbes that can cause diseases.

You need to have a tap and a hose that can be used to clean and fill this pond on a regular basis. You need to flush out all the water, scrub the pond and refill it whenever you feel like there is any debris in the water. If the water has an undesirable color or odor, it needs to be cleared out. Foaming is a sign that your pond needs some cleaning, as it could be home to fungi or other unwanted aquatic life.

It is always best to have natural ponds instead of the artificial ones. Of course, your space must permit that. In some of the popular Emu ranches and farms globally, entire water creeks have been created for the birds to enjoy and swim in. They also lend a lot of aesthetic appeal to the enclosure and the farm that houses the Emus.

Behavior enrichment accessories: Emus are extremely curious and inquisitive creatures. If you have had these birds as pets or have seen them on farms, you will notice that they are constantly attracted to jewelry, bangles, earrings or even watches.

It is good to encourage this curiosity in these birds as it is a source of entertainment and is a behavior enhancer. A disco ball, for instance, makes a great accessory in an Emu enclosure.

If you have grass as the substrate, make sure you have sprinklers installed, as your birds will simply love them. They will enjoy a shower or will just sprint through the mist. This is great exercise for them and of course, great entertainment for us.

In addition to that, you can add Kong toys that are filled with plastic bottles or small shiny objects. Leafy greens enclosed in ice blocks along with other food items make great foraging toys for the Emus.

2. Keeping the enclosure clean

There are large paddocks in Emu enclosures along with the substrate and the furniture that you may have installed including ponds, bushes, trees, logs and rocks. That is why it is extremely important to clean the enclosure completely. Usually, raking and scrubbing are the activities that you need to carry out on a regular basis. You may even have to replace the furniture in the enclosure from time to time.

You do not have to invest in a lot of chemicals to carry out these cleaning tasks. A little bit of water is usually enough to get rid of the dirt and debris. You will need a very small amount of detergent in case the enclosure is messier than you expect. After you have washed and rinsed off the items inside the enclosure with a hose, you need to make sure that it dries completely. This is done by placing them in the sun. This ensures that all the pathogens are killed off completely.

There is a schedule that you will have to carry out when it comes to keeping the enclosure clean. There are daily, monthly, weekly and annual cleaning activities that need to be carried out to maintain complete cleanliness.

For example, any man made pond will have to be cleaned out on a weekly basis. This requires you to empty them completely and then scrub them clean using a broom. Here is a schedule that you need to follow:

Raking: You need to rake the enclosure every alternate day. This includes the removal of any leaves, branches, leftover foods or feces. You can collect them into piles and then rake them into a wheel barrow or a bag for disposal.

Clean up the water dish: This needs to be done every day to ensure the best health of your birds. The water dish should be scrubbed clean using steel wool and should then be left to dry out in the sun. After that, you will have to refill it with clean water.

Cleaning the feeding dishes: The feeding dishes also need to be cleaned up every day. Hose it down and then scrub it clean with steel wool. Even this needs to be dried in the sun to get rid of the pathogens. It is a good idea to have a spare feeding dish that can be used when one is drying in the sun.

Cleaning the hay feeder: You need to have a hay feeder for your Emus. These feeders require weekly and monthly cleaning. You need to remove any hay from the bottom of the rack, remove cobwebs if any and also get rid of pests like spiders, rats and slugs every week.

The feeders should be pressure cleaned every month with water. Then, it needs to be dried in the sun. If you want to speed up the process of drying, you can even use a towel to dry the feeder.

Turning the substrate: This does not really have any time frame to carry out. You will have to clean out the substrate as and when needed. Using a pitchfork dingo digger or a shovel, this can be done quite easily. In case you plan to plant grass seeds, you will have to turn the substrate.

Replace the furniture in the enclosure: Every six months, it is recommended that you replace whatever furniture is present inside the enclosure. The logs, the rocks and even the behavior modification props can be replaced. You will need to decide based on the longevity of the accessory or the furniture in the enclosure before you change it. If something is made of plastic or other sturdy material and lasts long, you also have the option of replacing it annually.

Clear up all the browse pots: This must be done every week. The pots should be scrubbed neatly with steel wool. Water needs to be used with detergent only if there is too much debris. You can rinse the pots and sun dry them.

Clear out weed: This needs to be done whenever you feel like the weed growth is out of control. You can remove the weed by hand or even with proper weeding equipment. Since the weed is toxic to Emus sometimes, you need to take utmost care to clear them out.

Whenever you clean your Emu enclosure, you need to remember that nesting material of some sort should be left behind. If there is enough natural vegetation available, the birds will make use of it. If not, you will need to leave some material behind.

It does not matter if it is not the breeding season, usually between May and August, Emus may breed at any time as per their body clock.

a. Should you use any chemicals?
Cleaning up the cage may require the use of a disinfectant in case the routine cleaning process is not good enough for the birds. There are several products that are not only economical but also very safe for the birds as well as the keepers.

One of the products that is commonly used is Animal House. This can be used during the cleaning and scrubbing of the perches and the other accessories. This removes any blood, urine, oil or grease and even gets rid of dry feces.

This material is very safe to use and only requires gloves and glasses as protective equipment. Choose products that are biodegradable and non-residual in nature. You can look for products online or even contact popular Emu farms to understand what they are using for their enclosures.

It is important to disinfect any furniture in your Emu enclosure. In case Animal House is not easily available to you, you may even opt for a product called the F10Sc disinfectant. This veterinary disinfectant is also quite potent against the common microbes and works on a larger spectrum including fungi, viruses and bacteria. This is very eco-friendly and safe to use.

On small scale farms and backyard enclosures, chlorine is used as a disinfectant. This can be very harmful to the respiratory system of the bird and can even harm the people who are caring for the bird. It is best to use products that have been specially devised for Emu farms.

b. Pest control
This is one of the biggest concerns with respect to Emu enclosures. You need to make sure that your bird is not harmed by any of these pests that can carry several microbes and disease causing elements.

Some of these pests can also act as predators that are extremely harmful for your bird. Here are some of the common pests and ideas to keep them at bay:

Rodents: You can use any poison that is host specific to mice and rats. One option is Racumin. These products are targeted towards a certain pest and will not cause any secondary poisoning. You can even have stations with baits to trap these rodents. This can be an expensive option, as you will have to get several traps based on the size of your enclosure.

Fox Control: Fences are the best option for Fox control. Having a fox proof fence around the enclosure of your Emu works best in most cases.

Wild animal control: There are several wild animals that you will have to keep at bay including nocturnal animals and even ducks. These wild animals may steal the food meant for your Emu. In addition to that, they will also carry several disease causing elements. If you do not have any effective measure to control this in the initial stages, it can become a big hassle for you in the future. You will then have to remove the droppings and uneaten food left behind by these animals on a regular basis, mostly every day.

Controlling invertebrates: There are several invertebrates like slugs or snails that need not become a cause for worry, as your Emu will most likely eat them. However, there are other pests that you will have to keep at bay with Emu-friendly pesticides.

Once you have the enclosure in place and have made arrangements to maintain it, you can bring your Emus home. While the cost involved is much lesser in comparison to other farm animals, maintaining Emus requires a lot of time and also requires you to acquire the skills to handle these birds.

Chapter 3: Bringing the Emu Home

Emus are very easily available. You have the option of bringing home adult birds, chicks or even eggs. There are several Emu farms that thrive on supplying these birds to others. You can contact the Emu growers and breeders in your city or area. There are several options available for you to search for these individuals. You can contact the American Emu Association or even local Emu clubs for more information.

1. Buying your Emu

There are three options when it comes to buying your Emu.

Buying chicks: When you choose to bring an Emu home, you have the option of buying chicks in the hatching season that is usually in December. You will have to pre-order your chicks and place a deposit for every chick that you decide to purchase. Sales are usually limited and are really dependent upon the size of the farm. Even after the reservation has been made, your chicks will be kept on hold for about one week. A baby Emu is usually priced above $150-175 or £75-100. The chicks become more expensive as they age.

Buying fertile eggs: These beautiful blue eggs become available seasonally. Usually, the best season to pick up an Emu egg is late March or early November. The eggs are well wrapped and shipped to you in good condition. You will be able to insure your Emu egg against any possible breakage.

These eggs are quite large and need proper incubators. While none of the breeders will be able to guarantee that your eggs will have a live hatch, they will all be willing to lend you support in your incubation efforts and will even tell you how to purchase and set your incubator for best results.

Hatching the egg is a matter of chance. You may or may not have a pet Emu after the incubation period. When you purchase eggs, make sure that they have been laid after breeding an unrelated pair. Both the parent birds should have a history of hatchability and fertility in their previous clutches.

Buying or adopting adults: Buying an adult Emu is never recommended for a beginner. You will need to have good experience with respect to handling these birds. If not, there are chances that you will be hurt by the strong toenails and legs of these birds. They tend to kick and scratch, leading to serious injuries.

Adult Emus are extremely expensive with the cost of a pair going up to $21,000 or £10,000. This is usually a good option for individuals who are into the serious business of breeding and farming these birds. They will usually make a purchase when a highly fertile or good quality pair is available.

If you want an adult Emu, adoption is an option. These birds are rarely available in shelters, unless they have been rescued from a slaughter house. This is only possible if you are able to comply with all the requirements laid down by the adoption facility.

When you make a purchase from a breeder, whether it is an egg, a chick or an adult bird, you need to make sure that:

The birds are kept in large and clean enclosures with ample space for exercise and social interaction.
The birds are given good quality Emu feed.
The enclosure does not have too many rats or rodents.
The birds look healthy and clean.
The birds should have a curious disposition as opposed to a lazy and lethargic one.

It may be a good idea to visit a facility before you actually make a purchase, as these birds can be really expensive. It is always recommended that you opt for hand-raised chicks and adult birds as they tend to be easier to control. These birds are more accustomed to human company and will respond positively to new faces and people around them.

In case you have other farm animals or pets, you should make sure that they are kept in enclosures separate from these birds. Emus are very curious and docile, no doubt. However when they are startled or scared, they tend to attack quite aggressively.

Of course, the sheer size and the strength of the creature is an indication that you need to be very wary when introducing them to other pets or even children. They can cause serious injuries to both if there are any unpleasant interactions between them. You can try supervised interactions with growing chicks, but avoid these interactions with adult Emus as much as possible.

2. Keeping your records
It is never advisable to have a single Emu bird in your home. These birds require interaction and should be kept in pairs. Now, if you have the

space for it, you can even opt to keep these birds in communal groups. If you decide to have a group of Emus, you will have to maintain records of your bird to make sure that you are raising them correctly. There are a few things that you have to note down in complete detail:

Identification of the bird: This includes the scientific name of the birds, the names that you have given to them, the gender and other details such as band numbers. You will also have to note down any feature or mark that separates one Emu from the other.

This record may be made once in the Emu's lifetime. However, you can keep on recording the changes in the bird as they occur. For instance, the changes that occur from the juvenile to the adult stage. You will also have to keep updating any physical changes including injuries.

Parentage: Your breeder should be able to provide you with this information. You need to make a note of all the possible information about the parents of your Emu. You will have to include details such as the date of birth of the parents, whether they were wild or captive born, etc.

History: This is very important if you decide to bring home an adult Emu. You need to make a note of any information that is available about the bird. This includes details like the medical records, any specifications that can be provided by previous owners etc.

Current growing environment: Make a note of the type of habitat that you are providing your bird, the diet of your Emu, the other species that are being housed with your bird, the kind of water that you are providing your birds with, the disinfectants that you are using in the enclosure and other husbandry practices that you think are important.

Observations: You need to make a note of any marked pattern in the behavior of your Emus, the changes made in the diet of the bird, any unusual circumstances that the bird may have been exposed to or any form of stress that your bird may have experienced.

Veterinary exams: If you do take your bird to a vet, you need to note down the reason why you had to take the bird, the medicines that were administered, the treatment that was provided and details of any operations that were performed. It does not matter if your vet examination occurs weekly, monthly or annually, you need to keep a good record of it.

Reproductive stage: The condition of the bird, the behavioral changes when they reach the reproductive age, the matings that were sighted and the date of mating, the area where the nests have been located, the change in the diet and the number of eggs laid needs to be recorded. You also need to see how the nest of these birds have been created, whether they are in the way of the other bird's walking area or if they are susceptible to any damage by wild animals or the keepers themselves.

The movements: Emus are wanderers. The larger the space, the more they will wander. You will have to make a note of the areas that they visit frequently, the distance that they cover in a day and even changes that you make such as relocating an enclosure.

Size and weight of the birds: you need to record the height, the weight, the measurement from the bill to tail, the length of the limbs, the length of the neck etc. If you are hatching the eggs yourself, you need to take these readings as soon as the eggs have hatched or as soon as possible. In case of the chicks, you need to keep making these records every week to understand if your bird is growing well or not. Once they become juvenile, you can change the frequency to monthly. In case of adults, annual records are good enough.

Births and deaths: These records are necessary if you have several Emus on your farm. If any deaths have occurred within your flock, you have to note down the cause and even include the results of a post mortem, if conducted. You should also make a note of the births and include details like rejected eggs, the complications during egg laying etc.

Any other notable event: Attacks, escapes, pest control, supplement provision etc. should be noted down separately.

These records will help you understand the behavior of your Emus. Also, if you have to hire someone to take care of the birds in your absence, these records will be extremely useful for the new person.

It is believed that those who keep records of their Emus, whether the birds are raised commercially or as pets, tend to have better husbandry practices. This is purely because the records help you improve your knowledge tremendously.

They also play a vital role in research of your own. If you notice anything unusual, you can contact your vet immediately instead of realizing that it is too late to help your bird.

If you are looking at cooperative breeding which is a more commercial venture, you will have to maintain these records. They are often referred to as "studbooks". These books help trace back the origins of the bird and even help in finding the best possible specimens for the breeding programs.

3. Identifying your birds

This is very important for Emu owners and must never be taken lightly even if you have just two birds at home. Emus can be lured very easily and several people know the value of these birds. This means that theft of Emus can be a common problem that you will face as you raise your birds.

The most common identification method that is used is microchipping. These microchips are able to provide the best means of identification for the birds. They do not cause any harm to the birds. The microchips are inserted as soon as the eggs hatch in the pipping area just behind the bird's head. It is quite easy to do. A vet will be able to help you do this with a needle and an implant gun.

Of course, every type of technology comes with some disadvantages. Even with microchipping, there are a few issues, especially if you decide to have your bird microchipped after it has reached maturity.

You will have to provide an anesthetic to the bird. In addition to that, there is a risk of infection in the case of birds that have been injected. Catching the Emu and handling them for this process can also be quite difficult if you are dealing with grown or mature birds. If you are constantly trading and buying your birds from different sources, you cannot tell if the bird has been microchipped, visually. You will have to get into the details and the records etc.

The other option available is leg bands. They have long been used to identify poultry and farm animals. You will be able to get numbered leg bands that are also available in a lot of colors. This helps you distinguish between the birds, especially when you have a large group.

These bands are hazardous to the birds as they tend to get entangled quite easily. The birds, which are so curious by nature, will make it even worse by plucking at the band and trying to chew it.

The last identification method is tattooing. This has been used most successfully in these birds. It is a way of permanently identifying your birds, although it is not aesthetic. You also need to find a skilled expert who can do this without harming the bird.

Photo identification is an option, too, if you want to identify your birds to a certain extent. This is not feasible if you have a large group, as the birds look so similar to one another.

Chapter 4: Emu Care and Interactions

Once your birds have been purchased and the identification process is complete, you can get into the actual care details such as feeding the birds. Emus require a good deal of routine care in order to keep them healthy and in good shape. This chapter will tell you all about that and will even provide you with some fun bonding ideas with your birds.

1. Feeding your Emu

In the wild, Emus are omnivorous. This means that they will eat both plants and a few small animals, mostly slugs. But, even in the wild, these birds tend to rely on vegetation as the main source of food.

There are several plants that Emus relish in the wild including Sandalwood *Santalum,* Zamia palm and Quondong. In addition to this, they also indulge in young shoots of plants, native flowers, leaves, grass and seeds. If available, Emus also like to consume water plants like filamentous algae and duckweed. Dry material that forms the roughage is a very tiny part of the birds' diet.

These birds will eat small vertebrates like lizards. However, they mostly eat invertebrates like caterpillars, moths, slugs, sails, ants and crickets.

In some cases, these birds also consume droppings of other animals. If they notice any seeds in these droppings, the will peck the seeds out and consume them. While this may seem disgusting to most of us, it is a great way for the bird to consume food as the digestion process becomes much easier.

Emus do not have any teeth. That means that their food is not broken down before swallowing. To help in this process, these birds also swallow large pebbles. These pebbles help the bird macerate the food in the gizzard after it has been consumed.

In the Western part of Australia, a lot of research has been conducted on Emus that migrate. These birds show very similar food preferences, including seeds of the *Acacia anuera.* These seeds are consumed during the dry seasons.

After it rains, Emus prefer to eat grass or leaves from the Cassia tree. In spring, their diet consists mostly of grasshoppers and fruit from the Quandong tree.

Emus love to eat new types of food and will constantly look out for new options. Even if this means raiding nearby farms, the birds will not hesitate. They enjoy grains like barley and wheat that are cultivated on these farms.

a. Feeding in captivity

The diet of an Emu is quite different in captivity. To begin with, the variety that these birds are used to may not be available in captivity. In addition to that, it is recommended that you do not change the diet too often.

Your bird's diet should consist of a good mix of dry foods and fresh produce including fruits and vegetables. The only variety that should be provided is a change in the produce as per the season and the availability.

The diet of your Emu should ideally consist of:

Dry feed:

Pellets (poultry or goat pellets)
Cracked wheat
Grain mix including sorghum, barley and wheat
Puffed wheat
Lucerne Hay

You can feed about 1 kg of the grain mix per bird. You can also measure up about 6-8 cups per bird per day. As for the hay, you may give your Emu 1 biscuit of Lucerne hay each week per bird.

Fresh produce

The fresh produce given to your birds depends entirely upon the availability of the produce. The best options include:

Vegetables:
Green leafy vegetables like book choy, endives, Tuscan cabbage, dark lettuce, iceberg lettuce, chicory, sprouts, herbs, basil and rocket.
Whole broccoli
Whole cauliflower
Beans
Snow peas
Whole squash
Cut carrots
Cut zucchini

Fruits:
Grapes
Strawberries
Cherry tomatoes
Chopped apples
Raspberries
Chopped water melon
Chopped melons

Each bird will require at least one kilo of fresh produce every day. You can mix it up as per the availability and the preference of your bird.

b. Feeding references
For those who want to enter the business of Emus and want to raise them commercially, references from different zoos and wildlife parks might come in handy to provide proper nutrition for their birds. Emu farming is one of the most thriving businesses in Australia. In addition to that, several zoos and parks need to keep their birds in top condition for visitors to take a look at good, healthy specimens. They are the best point of reference for anyone who is interested in commercial Emu husbandry.

Here are three references for your Emu's diet from the most popular Emu farms and institutions in Australia.

Western plains zoo, NSW:

Approximately 1 kg of horse cube per Emu.
Access to natural vegetation and small insects in the enclosure.
Occasional treats such as fruits or nuts.

Hunter Valley Zoo, NSW:
Here the Emus are spread across the property and will share their housing space with other animals, too.

The diet consists of multipurpose pellets and a good mix of fruits and vegetables including tomatoes, grapes, leafy greens, pears, apples, rock melon and paw.

The birds are fed twice each day. This is because the housing is shared and the food may not be sufficient for both species.

Feed hoppers are used to provide the pellets. These hoppers are closed at night and opened again in the morning during the routine cleaning practices. This prevents vermin and wild animals from feeding on the pellets.

Browse, which is mainly leftovers from other animal enclosures, is a common food item presented to Emus. The browse from the day before is given to the birds, provided it is in good condition.

Vitamins and mineral supplements are not required as the birds are given multi-purpose pellets.

Australia Walkabout Wildlife Park, NSW
The Emus here free range on a land that spreads across 80 acres. They have access to seeds, flowers, insects, grass etc.

The birds are normally given macro pod pellets twice every day.

Food is given to these birds using a large trough.
Browse is always available to these birds.

There is no need to change the diet of these birds as they have the option of being free range.

These references can be of great help if you are looking for alternate diets for your Emus. However, depending upon the area available to you and the resources that are handy for you, you can chalk out a good diet plan for your birds with the help of your breeder and a vet.

c. The feeding routine
Preparing the diet for your Emu is a very easy task. You will have to scoop the dry feed into the buckets with the help of scoops that are available in most supply stores.

Fresh produce can be left whole or can be cut into small pieces. If you are planning to cut the produce, make sure that they are golf ball sized. Leafy greens that you provide to your bird need to be shredded. The enclosures should also have several rocks, pebbles and gravel to help in digestion.

You will have to feed your Emus at least once every day. This allows you to monitor the enclosure properly and even remove any dirt or debris. Try to keep the feeding area covered with a shelter. In case of any dampness or water, the dry food gets ruined. It may gather a lot of mold that is harmful for the birds.

Overfeeding the Emus is a common problem with most owners. The quantity mentioned above is only an average. If you find that your Emus are unable to eat the whole thing in a day, you should reduce the portions to just the right amount. If there is any food remaining in the enclosure, the Emus will not really over eat. However, these leftovers attract pests and wild animals.

It is important to clean the feeder and remove all the uneaten food before you top it up with new food. This prevents any rotten food from being consumed.

d. Supplementation
Usually, in a captive environment, supplements are not given to Emus. This is normally because the diet is designed to imitate their wild diet closely. The enclosure should have a lot of vegetation that will also attract invertebrates that your bird can easily feed on for additional nutrition.

You can purchase scientifically prepared pellets that are meant for Emus. Some popular brands include Riverina Emu pellets. These pellets will provide your bird with all the nutrition that is required for your bird.

Pellets make the best treats for the birds. If you have visitors on your farm or backyard, pellets can be fed out by them to interact with these birds. However, pellets are extremely expensive and are not necessary if the natural foods are good enough along with nutrition derived from foraging.

Supplements are usually given to birds that are raised commercially. This helps improve the quality of the meat, the leather and the oil of the bird.

In the breeding season you can improve the diet of the bird with supplements containing calcium carbonate and also multivitamins. You can ask your vet to prescribe these supplements to your bird. Never buy over the counter supplements for your pet Emus as it can lead to a lot of complications if it is not suitable to your bird.

e. Presenting the food
Presentation of the food is important to ensure that it is easy for the bird to access. You also need to provide enough protection to the food from weather conditions as well as predators.

When you are providing dry food, it is best to feed it through a covered feeder or dispenser. You can buy a covered feeder or even place a large trough under an overhead shelter.

There are several kinds of feeders that you can choose for your Emus. The rounded feeders are the best as they allow the bird to access the feed from different areas. That way, the aggression among the birds is reduced. This is the best option if you have a communal group of Emus.

The rounded feeders have separate slots for the birds to stick their head in and eat. You also have a round slot from above that allows you to refill the trough every day as required.

You can have large troughs created especially for the fresh produce. The Emus can access this easily and may feed from it whenever they want. These troughs also allow many birds to eat at one time, making it the most convenient option.

If you have fewer birds, you can even give them individual trays that are scattered around the ground. Keep changing the position of the individual troughs to make feeding time more entertaining for the birds. Once in a week, you may want to scatter the fruits all over the enclosure, not in trays, to make it a fun activity for your bird.

Normally, providing hay in a trough is an option. However, you may want to purchase hay feeders, as it will keep other animals at bay. Since hay is not replaced on a daily basis, it is also maintained better and protected from moisture and dirt when placed in a feeder.

You will have to place large water troughs with fresh and clean water for your birds to access easily. This trough should be kept under a shelter. It is advised that you have this trough cleaned up on a daily basis to maintain the quality of the drinking water. If there are ponds, you may catch your birds drinking out of it from time to time. Nevertheless, you have to provide a separate drinking trough for your bird.

Any supplement that is recommended should be given to your bird by mixing it with the water or the food.

f. Food for enrichment

Feeding can become a great activity for your bird when you get creative with food presentation. Your bird can get a lot of enrichment when the task of getting the food becomes a little more challenging for your bird. Here are a few ways you can present food for enrichment:

You can hang fruits like grapes on the trees. This makes the birds stretch in order to reach them and makes it a great physical activity for your Emu.

You may choose to hang up leafy greens on trees. However, the birds may not notice them among the foliage. So, you can even hang the greens on the fence enclosures.

Cut fruits like watermelon in half and scatter them around the enclosure. The birds will find them, peck at them and eat out of these fruits.

The fruits or the vegetables should be placed in trees that have low forks so that the Emu can reach and pluck them out.

Chop fruits up into large cubes and scatter them around.

You can tie carrots with ropes and hang them up on a tree. This gives the birds the task of untying the knot and getting the carrots out.

You can look for blunt hammer stakes and tie a few leafy greens to it using a rope. This is also a great foraging activity.

Stockings filled with grass seeds can be hung down from trees. As the grass grows through the stockings, your Emus can eat out of them. Since the stocking will swing or blow around due to the wind, the Emus will have a challenge of some sort.

Feeding the bird and providing them with some form of recreation through food can be a great bonding activity. If your birds look forward to the feeding session, he will also most likely learn to obey commands and will be trained easily.

2. Declawing

Declawing is a rather important decision that you will have to take when it comes to your Emus. If you are raising chicks on your farm, especially, declawing might become an important decision to make.

Now, this is a safety measure that you can take if you are going to have several visitors on your farm. Declawing is known to also change the behavior of the birds quite drastically, making them less aggressive with people and with one another.

Declawing is a practice that is becoming increasingly popular on farms in Australia. The objective is to reduce the chances of any damage to the skin of other birds in case any aggressive behavior is depicted. The primary benefit of declawing is the economic value. Losses of close to $5 million are prevented by declawing birds and reducing injuries to the hide.

However, this subject is controversial. Most Emu farmers believe that this process can lead to a lot of discomfort and pain to the birds. Normally, to ensure that the claws do not grow back, the distal phalangeal bone is removed. This causes severed nerves and a lot of damage to the tissues surrounding the area. When the surgery is not performed correctly, it can even lead to nerve damage resulting in increased sensitivity to stimuli.

There is another major concern with respect to declawing, which is the formation of neuromas that are very painful. When they occur, they persist all through the life of the Emu. They can appear in the form of masses of disintegrated nerves or may develop as small fascicles scattered across the leg.

All birds are digitigrade creatures. This means that they walk on their toes mostly. In the case of large birds like the Emu, the number of toes are reduced and there is also a large amount of stress on them. If the toes are partially removed, chances are that the gait of the bird will be heavily compromised. There is no evidence to support this, however.

The only thing that has been noticed is that there is a significant difference in the size of the left and right footprint in case of birds that are declawed. This is not a very statistically significant reading. However, this can explain the formation of a rudimentary claw in some Emus.

In some cases, Emus that have been declawed tend to become flat footed. The total area of the footprint is a lot bigger in comparison to the birds that have all the claws intact. There are videotapes and even images of the footprints to suggest that the birds that are declawed have a significantly more flat-footed gait.

a. Behavioral changes in the birds
The behavior of the Emus that were declawed have been studied using videotapes. They studied discrete behavior and timed behavior of the bird. The different behaviors that were studied included:

Inactive behavior: This includes the way the birds sit, stand or just rest. There were no marked changes in this type of behavior in case of birds that had been declawed. The only difference that was noticed was that birds who have been declawed do not stand up as much as birds that are not declawed.

41

Ingestive behavior: This includes foraging, drinking, eating and elimination of waste. While the clawed and declawed birds showed very little variation in their ingestive behavior, it was noted that declawed birds had lesser eating bouts in comparison to clawed birds.

Change position: This includes the shift of positions when the bird is sitting, when the bird is moving to a standing position to a sitting one or vice versa. In this case, there was no difference noticed at all.

Grooming and social behavior: this includes behaviors like preening, the head scratch, fence peak, stretch, head through the fence, the head shake etc. The groups that were clawed showed more typical behavior than the ones that were declawed. For example, they would poke their heads in through the fence and interact with other birds a lot more. This behavior was less frequent in case of declawed birds.

Aggressive behavior: This includes behavior such as pecking, step pushing, chasing, running away, thrusting and response to any aggressive behavior. Clawed birds showed more instances of step pushing, thrusting and pecking. It was seen that declawed birds were less aggressive in comparison to their clawed counterparts.

Locomotor behavior: this includes walking, searching, pacing, running and pace of running. Pacing and running was significantly lesser in case of birds that were declawed.

In case you have large groups of Emus, it may be beneficial to declaw the birds as the social structure improves significantly with the reduction in aggression. However, if you have trained your birds sufficiently and have made them social, it is a good idea to avoid declawing altogether.

To prevent aggression, it is recommended that you never try to bond two birds after the age of 12 months as they become extremely territorial and protective about their space.

3. Training the Emu

Emus are good companion birds. They are docile and friendly if they have been raised from a young age. In fact, they tend to imprint upon people. This means that if you are the first thing that baby bird sees after hatching, he is likely to believe that you are his mommy. This will make him follow you around and be extremely loving towards you.

That said, is it possible to train Emus? Well, it is something that you can try if you have ample time and patience. However, not many have been successful in training these birds. There are a few things that you can teach your Emu to do with patience and practice.

a. Harness training

Harness training an Emu is not just a bonding activity that can help you make good pets out of your Emus. This is actually a safety measure that you can take for your birds when you are raising them.

You can use D type dog harnesses on young Emus in order to begin your training process. Since these birds are much larger than dogs, you may want to use a horse harness or a specially designed harness on your bird for safety and comfort.

Now, Emus are not easy to train for walking with a harness. These birds, when they are adults, are especially hard to handle and work with. They tend to kick around and may even bite or peck at you when you try to put a harness on them.

It is always better to begin with juveniles. You can put the harness around the bird and just prompt him or her to walk with you. You can use a treat to begin the training. If the birds have been imprinted with you, they will follow you around and will try to walk with you without any difficulty.

One important thing to remember when you are training Emus to walk with a harness is that these birds cannot walk backwards. They can only move forward. So, when you provide any resistance from the harness, they will either panic and get completely spooked or will simple lay down upon resistance. You need to alter the intensity of the restraint to tell the bird that you want them to stop.

You can even use a cue such as "stop" every time you try this. If the bird responds with a proper stop, give him or her a treat. You need to make sure that you do not tug at the Emu too hard when you are doing this.

In case you want to harness an adult bird, you need to learn the right way to restrain the bird in the first place. This is discussed in complete detail in the following chapter. Only when you have mastered this should you venture into handling the bird and trying to place a harness on it.

There are several reasons why harness training can be useful for Emu owners:

If the bird shelter is located away from the free-range area, it may become difficult to get the birds back into their shelters. Harness training them helps you lead the birds back at the end of the day.

As discussed before, Emus wander and can get lost very easily. If someone finds your bird, they will be able to handle it easily when the bird has been trained on a harness.

It is a great activity to bond with your Emus, as they will love to spend some quality time with you.

Birds that are harness trained tend to be more friendly and cooperative. They will also respond a lot better to strangers when they have been properly trained.

Harness training is something that you need to try if you are raising chicks. It helps when you are transporting the birds, trying to get them to a vet or just shifting them from one enclosure to the other.

b. Training them to respond to calls
This is a fun training activity with your birds. When you train them to respond to your calls, it helps to:

Get them into the shelters at night.
Find them when they have wandered away from the enclosure.
Get them to come to you when you want to examine them or just play with them.

The best time to train a bird to respond to your calls is during their feeding sessions. That is when you can actually get the attention of your birds. The first thing to do is to make a lot of noise every time you refill the feeding troughs. This alerts the birds and makes them curious towards what is happening in the enclosure.

Then, after you have prepared the food for the Emus, make a very obvious call. If you have just two birds, you can call the names out quite loudly. If there are many birds, you can use calls like "Here Birdy". When the birds come to you, you can present the food bucket to them.

Eventually, the bird will come to you whether you give them their food or not. Of course, the occasional treat will help them remember these commands. Unlike dogs or cats, Emus are not the best at remembering the training that is given to them.

You will have to make constant reinforcements by presenting the food bucket or giving the bird a treat.

c. Training them to wait

Yes, it is possible to train an Emu to wait for you or stop a certain activity. However, unlike a dog, the wait command is not something that you can control. You can restrain the bird from doing something you do not approve of for a maximum of 2 minutes. After this, they will get back to their own ways.

A sharp and loud "No!" when your bird does something undesirable will stun or startle the bird for a second. The bird takes some time to come out of this state. In that time, you can give your bird a treat.

Increase the time between the command and the presentation of the treat to help your bird learn what the command means and wait for a longer time. Eventually, a treat will not be needed at all.

There are other things that people train the Emus to do such as pulling carts and riding them. However, you need to be very careful with this, as the birds cannot take too much weight.

Ostrich riding is a popular sport. These birds are sturdier and stockier, weighing about 500 lbs. But the Emu is not as heavy and cannot lift as much weight. In fact, the bird will lay down when too much weight is placed on them.

In some parts of the world, making an Emu pull carts or riding them is considered cruelty. In fact, a man from Queensland was recently pressed with legal charges for riding an Emu and posting pictures of it on social media!

Chapter 5: Handling and Transporting Emus

Learning to handle an Emu correctly can help you prevent a lot of injuries and can even reduce stress on your birds to a large extent.

Emus will have to be transported occasionally even if you are not raising them for commercial purposes. You will have to learn to transport your bird to take them to the vet, get them to new enclosures etc.

The first step is to learn how to handle these birds. There are various techniques and equipment that you can use to get a hold of your Emu. While they are easier to handle when they are younger, they can be quite a handful when it comes to adults.

1. Capturing and handling

You need to make sure that you time the capture time of the bird to ensure that the bird is not adversely affected. You see, the first time a bird is captured or handled is very stressful for the bird. This can make them exert a lot of energy just to get away from you. What happens due to this is that the bird may have a bout of overheating if you time the capture for a time of the day that is already too hot.

a. Best time to catch the Emu

The best time to capture your bird is early in the morning. This is the time of the day that is usually quite cool. Even late afternoons are feasible for the birds as it is not too hot.

You can use certain tools or even use food as a bait to condition your birds. Using food makes the birds look at the capture as a positive experience. They can be easily enticed with a few treats to walk into the transport boxes.

Capturing the birds at night is also a great idea as the birds are less active and will actually be less resistant to the capture. You can even approach the bird easily as their visibility is quite low at night. The birds will not even know when you are approaching them and it is less likely that they will get startled and run away from you. They will also not have enough time to react or respond if you secretly approach them at night.

When you are planning the capture, make sure that there are no people around the bird. To begin with, the sight can be disturbing to many. In addition to that, if the bird tries to run away, it may harm someone else who accidentally gets in the way of the bird.

If you plan to have your bird transferred to a new facility, the best time to capture him or her is early in the morning. That way, the birds will be able to adjust to the new surroundings or enclosures quite easily before sunset.

In case you are planning to send the bird over to a facility that is quite far, requiring overnight travel, you may want to capture the bird in the afternoon. This gives the bird ample time to adjust to the transport vehicle or box. They will also be more comfortable as night times are cooler and more comfortable for the bird.

They will also arrive at the new destination at sunrise the next day, making it easy for them to adjust to their new surroundings.

Make it a point to avoid capture and transport during the breeding season. This is when the birds are more temperamental. This makes it harder for you to get hold of the bird. It is very disturbing for the Emus and will make them even more resistant to the whole experience than ever before.

You must never try to capture or handle an Emu that is sick or injured. This increases stress for the bird. In some cases the attempt to capture and handle can be fatal for the birds. If it is necessary to get hold of the birds to take them to the vet, you can do so, taking extra care not to startle the bird.

You must never try to capture a bird several times on the same day. This puts a lot of stress on the bird. In case the bird gets too aggressive or agitated from the first attempt, just give him or her a break and get back to the regular routine with your Emu.

You can try again the next day after giving your bird ample time to recover from the stress of the first capture. This time you can try a new approach or technique. Even changing the time of capture can be very helpful in restraining the bird and catching them by complete surprise.

What you need to remember is that every capture should be very well planned. If it is not organized, the process will be very messy. You can avoid overexertion because of long chases. You can even look for the best temperature and weather conditions to find the perfect ambience to catch your bird.

It is not only about stressing the bird out. If the temperature goes over 27 degrees and the bird is still being chased around, he can even succumb to hyperthermia and overexertion.

There are several cases when Emus simply drop dead form being chased around the cage despite unfavorable weather conditions. This is the result of unplanned capture sessions in most cases.

b. Techniques to catch Emus

There are many methods that you can use to easily catch these birds. They are, as we discussed before, very easy to lure into boxes or restraint areas.

Using catching bags

It is a good idea to use a large sack such as a hessian sack in order to restrain the bird after it has been caught. This is the best option if the transport distance is short.

You need to make sure that the bag is made of some strong and sturdy material such as hessian. Remember that the claws of these birds are very sharp and can just tear through material that is lighter and less sturdy.

When you restrain the bird with a sack, make sure that you only have the legs and the body inside the bag. The head and the neck should stick out to keep the bird from panicking.

You will need a bag with a standard dimension of 100 cm X 60 cm. This is good enough for younger Emu birds. This technique is usually avoided on birds that are larger in size.

Before you get into the other techniques of capture and restraint, you need to make sure that you understand that Emu capture is a risky process. There are several dangers involved and you need to be completely aware of what you are getting into. Even a bird that is not very aggressive generally can become entirely different when they realize that you are trying to catch them. Here are a few things that you need to keep in mind at all times:

The legs of the bird are extremely sturdy. Your clothing should be made of material that is not very easy to tear or damage.

It is recommended that you wear long sleeved garments and full-length trousers to protect yourself.

Safety glasses are a must as the birds can peck at your eyes or may poke at it using their claws while struggling to get away from you.

Gloves are a must as the legs of the bird are quite rough. They are almost like sandpaper and will damage bare hands.

Once you are fully geared up, you can try one or more of the following techniques to catch your Emu successfully.

The right way to catch the bird

If you need to move an Emu over a short distance, the most important tool that you need is food. In most cases, that is all you will need to lead your bird towards a facility for capture or into a transport box.

If your bird has been harness trained, you can easily approach an Emu and restrain it without much resistance from the bird. You will not even have to chase the bird around too much if you walk up to the bird in the right way and capture it.

You will not require any nets or harnesses in most cases as you can hold the Emu in a manner that allows you to restrain it. Only when you have to get hold of the bird in an emergency will a net come in handy. Of course, you would require really large nets. You need to be extra cautious not to hurt the bird.

You need to follow the following methods to capture the bird, as recommended by experienced Emu keepers:

Always approach the bird from behind like you are going to give it a big bear hug. Then, catch the body of the bird and try to get on top of the bird.

Exerting pressure downwards is necessary. Emus will not try to get up if there is a lot of pressure on their backs. If they feel any weight, they will stay on the ground.

Then, hold the legs of the bird and pull them up towards the body of the bird.

It is recommended that you use two people for this technique. One person can easily be swung aside by this bird. You see, Emus will try to free their legs first and will give you dangerous kicks that can be quite painful and harmful as well.

Transport box capture

This method may seem like it is straight out of a cartoon film but it works like a charm on Emus. Here are a few steps to help you get the bird into a capture box without any chasing or struggle:

49

Scatter food around the enclosure, leading to the transport box. This will get the interest of the Emu instantly.

The bird will actually follow the line of the food and walk into the box.

Keep a bowl of food inside the cage to keep the bird engaged after it has stepped into the box.

Then you can slide the door onto the transport box quite easily. Make sure you are quick in doing this. The bird should be well into the box so that you do not cause any damage to the body of the bird.

If you see that the bird is lingering around and is not really getting into the box, you can give him a slight push to get him into the box.

Using this method from the time your bird is a chick will condition him or her to the box and will make it less stressful and a lot easier on the bird.

When you want to capture a chick, here are a few things to keep in mind:

The box should be lined with hay or any other soft floor material.
Keep food and water bowls inside the box so that the bird does not feel scared or out of place.

You can lure chicks into the box just like an adult. They will walk into the box, crouch down on finding the food and will sit down to enjoy the meal.

It is much easier to lure chicks into these boxes, as they are not very hesitant or cautious. They are easier to manipulate than the adult birds.

This type of capture is considered the best as it is less stressful for the bird and the person who is trying to handle the bird. You should be able to talk to your breeder to find good quality transport boxes for your birds.

These boxes will have several holes on the surface. This allows the box to be well ventilated and will let your bird breathe without any problems.

Try to make capture methods as comfortable for the bird as possible. Providing treats, making sure that he has enough water to drink and even talking to the birds in a calm and gentle voice will make them less afraid the next time you need to repeat the whole process.

On the other hand, if you injure the bird the first time or just scare them too much, they will always run away from you when you try to approach them.

c. Techniques to restrain

It is quite easy to restrain Emus that are young and up to 5kg in weight. All you need to do is fold the leg and hold the bird close to your own body. The Emu juveniles have a tendency to defecate when you do this. So it is necessary that you keep the vent away from your body and clothing.

It is not a good idea to force birds that are heavier into this folded leg position. You can let their legs dangle while you hold the body.

To restrain an adult Emu, hold the bird with one hand, supporting the chest of the bird. Then take your other arm over and hold the upper leg of the bird.

In this position, you can lift the bird right off the ground while you keep the legs away from your own body.

You need to make sure that you are comfortable with a certain bird before you try to restrain it or hold it. If the Emu is somewhat docile and calm, you will be able to walk up to the bird and just hold it. These birds may not even struggle as you attempt to lift them off the ground.

However, if one of the birds has a history of being unpredictable and aggressive, it is a good idea to find a helper to restrain the bird.

There is another hold that you may try with adult Emus. While you keep one arm below the bird, you will have to grasp the wings with the free hand.

Keep the legs pointed away from your body as you lift the bird. This is a simple hold for one person. You also should be strong enough to carry a bird as massive as the Emu. If you do not have the physical ability to grasp the bird, you will sustain serious injuries and wounds.

If you want to get into a standing restraint with your Emu, you will have to approach the bird from behind and catch hold of the short wings. The tail must be straddled while the wings are held close to the body.

This type of restraint is mostly used for examination purposes, mostly to determine the gender of the bird.

Restraining a baby Emu is much easier. All you have to do is hold the baby against your body with the legs folded up. This is the most effective method of restraining your bird. In some cases you may have to support the neck of the bird. This can be done when the bird is struggling to get free or is trying to jump off.

Keeping one hand free will allow you to carry out any procedure such as examining your bird or administering recommended medicines to the bird.

When you are going to the release the bird, just lower it onto the ground gently. You should make sure that your bird is able to feel the ground before you release him. This gives him a sense of security.

Chemical restraint is never required for most Emus. These birds are easy to handle if they have been trained well enough. Chemical restraint is only required when the birds need immediate veterinary help or if the bird is becoming overtly aggressive.

There are also some diagnostic procedures that require the bird to be completely immobile. In such cases, you can administer an inhalant anesthetic such as isoflurane. This is administered using a mask. It is the safest type of chemical restraint as the recovery is also rapid.

You have to always bear in mind the strength of the bird when you decide to restrain it or even try to handle it. The larger the bird, the more assistance you may need with your Emu.

If you are raising Emus in your backyard, it would help you a great deal if another family member is involved closely in the care of the Emus. They should know all the restraining procedures and the capturing techniques to help you with the bird.

d. Examining Emus

It is necessary to examine your Emu from time to time to understand if there are any skin lesions, lumps or injuries on the body of the bird.

You can use any of the restraining methods mentioned above to examine your birds. Holding the bird with the legs up works the best. This is when having a helper will come in handy. While one holds the bird, the other may carry out the examination.

In most cases, having one more person who can hold the head and the legs of the bird is necessary to conduct examinations. This prevents the bird from moving around too much and will make it a lot easier to check your bird properly.

In case a certain examination procedure is prolonged, it is absolutely necessary to have another person to help you. You may even need to chemically restrain the bird in some cases. In these cases, holding the bird down to the ground while examining it is the best option available to you. They are more at ease. This is also a more comfortable position for you. Remember, it is not easy to hold a big bird in your arms for too long.

Weighing your bird

There are several reasons for weighing your Emus. You will have to check if the birds are growing up as planned or not. You also need to be able to weigh the birds during the breeding season or if the bird is recovering from a longstanding illness.

There are two simple ways to weigh the bird. First, you may restrain your Emu and step on the weighing scale with the bird. Then, subtract your weight to get the weight of your Emu.

You can also lure the bird into a box and follow the same process of weighing the bird in the box and then subtracting the weight of the box.

It is possible to use food and condition your Emu to step up on a Weighing Scale. This is not an easy task to do as Emus tend to take long hours of practice to master these tricks. However, this is the most stress free option available as far as Emu weighing goes.

e. Releasing your bird
Releasing your Emu is just as tricky as restraining the bird. You need to keep a few pointers in mind to ensure that your bird is successfully released without any compromise on the safety of the bird. Here are a few things to keep in mind:

The birds should be released in the morning if they have been transported to a new enclosure. Even after restraining them for long examinations, it is a good idea to release the bird in the morning. This keeps the bird cool and will also give you the chance to keep an eye on the bird. The birds will also have the whole day to recover.

When you release the bird into its enclosure, you need to make sure that water and food is available. If it is a new enclosure, you will have to clear the space of any cartons, boxes or unwanted obstacles as the birds will just run right into them. You must also release the bird into an area of the new enclosure that has the maximum amount of open space.

Keep an eye on the bird after its release. You will have to keep an intermittent check on the bird all day to make sure that it is ok. Is the bird behaving normally? Is the breathing alright? Is the bird stressed by the capture?

As soon as you have determined that the bird is in good health, you can allow the bird to join the other Emus in your enclosure, if any.

Even after the bird is released into the common holding area, you will have to look for possible signs of aggression among the birds. If you notice any behavioral change in the bird that has been released or the other birds, you may have to bring the new bird out for safety reasons. It does not matter if the bird has bonded with the rest of the Emus already.

The next tricky thing to do is getting the bird transported. Whether it is a short distance trip to the vet or a long distance one to a new ranch or a new home, you need to take all the necessary steps to keep your bird safe.

2. Transporting your Emu

There are several requirements when it comes to transporting an Emu. One option is to look for airlines that can provide cargo services to have your bird transported. In case of intercontinental transport, you will have to check with the wildlife authorities of the destination to understand the laws governing Emu transport.

More likely, you will have to transport your bird by car. There are several requirements that you will have to fulfill to make sure that your bird is being transported safely. The primary transport requirements are:

a. The box design

You need to maintain the following parameters to ensure that your transport box is entirely safe for your Emu to be shipped or taken by road:

The material: You need to have sturdy material such as synthetic, fiberglass, heavy duty plastic, which is 3 cm in diameter, or wood.

Size: The box must allow freedom of movement for the bird. The containers should allow the bird to stand up erect, turn fully or lie down. This is the only movement that should be possible. If you get a box that is too big, there are chances that the bird will hurt itself. You need to make sure that there is a clearance of 10 cm above the head when the bird is standing.

The frame: the frame should be made of solid wood on both sides and should have a base that is nailed into place or screwed into position to prevent any damage.

The sides: It is recommended that the sides of the box are made from plywood that is 2cm in thickness. You may use any other material that can match the strength of this material. In case you are using net or slats on the upper part of the box, the plywood side must reach the upper body of the bird. You should make sure that the insides of the container do not have any sharp protrusions.

Handles or handler spacers: You will need to have a spacing block on all four sides of the container. This should be at least 2.4cm in thickness. There should be a forklift spacer bar if the contents of your box weigh more than 60kg.

The floor: The flooring of the box should also be made of plywood of 2cm thickness. You also need to make sure that the floor has a non-slip covering to protect the bird.

The roof: The roof can have netting or can be solid. You may even opt for a mixed roof. You need to make sure that it is lined with some padding that is non-destructible. You may use foam rubber. This is required, as Emus tend to jump up. You can also use some material that contains light over the netting to prevent any nervousness in your Emus.

The door: It is best to use a sliding door as it can be closed and opened easily and even fast enough to keep the bird restrained. You have to provide the option of screwing the door into place after it is closed. There must be strengthening battens on the door of the transport box.

Ventilation: If you are using solid material for the box, you will have to make ventilation openings. These openings should at least be 2.5 cm in diameter. They should cover about 20% of the whole area of the box. They need to be placed on all four sides mandatorily. The lower openings need to be at least 5cm above the bedding area to prevent any type of spillage. You can even cut the corners of the partitions to allow better circulation of air.

b. Furnishing and accessories
For most birds, furnishing inside the transport box can reduce a lot of stress. You will have to include some in your Emus box as well. Here are a few furnishing guidelines that you may follow:

Perches are not required for Emus.

You need to add some form of bedding such as wood shavings. This needs to be placed above a thick layer of newspaper that is at least 2.5 cm in thickness. You can use any other absorbent material of your choice. The bedding should be placed at a depth of about 10 cm.

c. Food and water
If the bird has access to food and water during its transport experience, chances are that the levels of stress will be reduced tremendously. You also need to allow the birds to have an ample supply of food to maintain their health during the transport. Here are a few guidelines for the food and water requirements:

The water container and the food container should be placed at floor level. They should be accessible from the outside in case they need to be refilled.

The water containers should have a diameter of at least 30 cm to make it easily accessible to the bird.

You need to insert a sponge inside the water container to make sure that there is no spillage.

You need a flanged water container.

You will not have to provide the bird with any additional watering or feeding within 24 hours from the time they have been shipped or dispatched.

In case the bird needs to be fed due to any delay or unforeseen conditions, you need to make sure that there are carrots or apples placed in each compartment of the container.

d. Space per Emu
When you are transporting Emus, you need to make sure that the birds have ample space. There are some guidelines that you will have to maintain. Usually not more than six birds should be transported as a group. The space required depends, however, on the age of the bird. This is the reference that you will need when you plan to transport your birds:
1 to 2 day old chicks: They will need a box that measures 51X45X23cm.

Adults: You will have to get a communal container that allows at least 0.44 square meters per bird.

e. The right time of transportation

The timing that you choose to transport your bird depends entirely upon the distance that the bird will have to travel.

In the case of short distances: You should transport the birds early in the morning so that they reach their destination while there is enough sunlight. This allows these birds to get accustomed to their new surroundings.

In case of long distances: The birds should be captured either in the morning or in the afternoon. Thereafter, you will have to leave the bird in the transport box for a while to ensure that he or she gets used to the space. Make sure that the health of the bird is well monitored while it is in the box. It is best to carry out long distance transports at night, as the birds are calmer. You also have the advantage of less activity on the part of the birds.

f. Releasing after transport

You need to make sure that your birds are released into their new space correctly. This can help reduce stress to a large extent and will also make the birds happier in their new surroundings:

If the bird has been transported interstate or overseas, the first thing to keep in mind is that the bird should be released into a quarantining area. This will prevent the spreading of diseases among the flock.

If the bird is being released into an empty enclosure, you will only have to place the container in the area and open the door. The best time to do this is early in the morning. When the bird is ready, he will leave the container himself. You will have to make sure that the bird is given enough food and water and is monitored all day long.

If the bird is being released into an enclosure that is inhabited by other birds, you can follow the same method as above. You only have to make sure that the transport box is placed in the holding area that is usually adjacent to the main enclosure.

These release methods will also help you when you have your bird shipped in to your farm or home. It helps the bird understand the new surroundings and get used to them.

Chapter 6: Health Requirements of Emus

Keeping your Emus in their best shape is your responsibility. You can find an exotic animal vet or an avian vet to help you in the process of Emu health management. You will be able to get several references from Emu farms or on websites like www.aav.org.

1. Keeping a daily check

A health check is required on a daily basis with your Emu. These are distant checkups just to keep an eye on the birds. You need to ask yourself the following questions while carrying out these routine checkups:

Are the birds able to move around freely? Are they able to use their legs properly without the evidence of any swelling, bumps or lacerations?

Are the birds feeding normally or are they overeating? How easily are they able to swallow the food down their throats?

Are they able to drink water properly? Is there any sign of excessive consumption of water?

Are all the feathers of the bird intact? Is there any evidence of knotted up feathers, matted down feathers or bald patches?

Are the droppings of the birds normal in their consistency or can you see any traces of blood or spots?

Do you see any discharge near the eyes, the cloacal region or the beak of the bird?

How are they moving the neck? Are the movements comfortable or do the birds show signs of bumps and lacerations?

How is the behavior of the birds? Is it normal or have the birds done anything that is out of character for them?

If you have a positive response to all the questions above, there are no immediate health concerns. However, it is necessary to carry out detailed health examinations to be sure that your bird is in good health.

2. Detailed examinations

Like we discussed before, it is quite easy to examine Emus by just restraining them temporarily. Chemical restraint is not really necessary for these birds as they are fairly docile in nature.

You may have to opt for chemical restrain in case there are any surgical processes that need to be carried out. In this case, it is necessary for a vet to be present for the examination. You need to provide a dosage of the chemical based on the weight of the bird.

In case there is a need to chemically restrain the bird, you can take the opportunity to carry out other physical examinations that would be too difficult otherwise. It may also be a little dangerous to venture into detailed physical examination under normal conditions. You can check the oral cavity, the vent or the ears when the bird has been sedated.

a. Physical examination

When an Emu has been physically restrained, it is fairly easy to carry out the following examinations:

Weight:

You can use the two methods mentioned in the previous chapter to check the weight of the bird.

Take a look at the difference in the weight of the bird based on the record. You need to understand if the weight has increased or decreased or just remained consistent.

You also have to check the bones of the bird to make sure that the bird has no protrusions. In addition to that, when you hold the bird, you should be able to feel all its muscles properly.

Eyes:

The eyes should be alert and bright.

Discolorations, accumulations or scars must be noted down.

There should be no blood or scab formation around the eyes of the bird.

The sight can be tested by waving something shiny before the bird. If he reacts to the object by ducking or by pecking at it, you can be sure that his eyesight is pretty good.

Beak:

Check the beak closely and make sure that there is no discharge around the nostrils of the bird.

There should not be any crusty formation near the nostrils of the bird.

If the beak has any deformity or seems unusually shaped, you need to take note of it immediately.

Make sure you smell the nostrils of the Emu. If there is any unpleasant odor, it is a matter of concern.

You should also watch out for any wheezing sound or abnormal sound from the nostrils of the Emu.

Oral Cavity:

Make sure you look for any discharge, unpleasant odor or accumulation in the oral cavity.

There should not be any lesion in the oral cavity.

The mucous membrane should be of a normal color.

You will have to check the upper palate in the oral cavity. If there is any accumulation in his area, it is an indication of respiratory issues.

Respiration:
The bird should not show any signs of wheezing or crackling while breathing. Coughing or sneezing is also an indication of an impending problem with respiration.

Skin and feathers:
The skin should be normal in its color.

You should not be able to see any swellings or lesions on the skin of the bird.

Scabs, inflammations, dry skin and other abnormalities should be noted down immediately.

The plumage and the skin should be examined for any mites, lice or other ectoparasites. You also need to make sure that there are no signs of a recent occurrence of these parasites on the body of the bird.

Look for any missing feathers or patches on the body of the bird.

Run the fingers throughout the body of the bird and make not of feather breakages or bleeding in the feathers.

Body:
Check the whole body for any chances of abnormalities, bumps or lesions.

There should not be any tenderness in the legs of the birds or in their necks. You can run your hand on these areas and apply a little pressure. There should not be signs of discomfort upon the application of light pressure.

Examine the wings of the bird carefully and check if there are any fractures or other restrictions such as paralysis of the wing. The wings should be able to move easily.

Check the feet of the bird and see if all the claws are intact. Any sign of bumps or lesions must be noted down immediately.

The vent:
The vent of the bird should be carefully examined to understand the health of the gastrointestinal tract of the bird.

If there are any parasites or signs of soiling of the feathers you will have to look into it immediately.

Any swelling, redness, diarrhea or evidence of egg laying is considered an abnormality that needs to be taken care of
immediately.

Dryness, cracking, smelly discharge, dried feces and abnormally colored feces should be noted down too.

b. Routine tests and treatments
Your Emus should receive routine treatments at regular intervals. Most common health issues can be prevented if your birds get routine treatments and tests along with good husbandry practices. Here are a few

routine treatments that you will have to perform on the bird yourself or with the assistance of a vet:

The birds should be wormed with the help of a broad spectrum wormer. This process should be carried out one in three months or as advised by the vet. There are several worming products that contain Levamisole. These are normally recommended for your Emus. You need to make sure that you consult your vet before using any products to worm your birds. You can even contact the manufacturers in case you want to practice off label use of these products. This consultation is mandatory to understand the dosage required and how the wormer should be administered.

Check the feces every six months. You will have to look for traces of worm eggs or protozoa.

Birds should be tested for salmonella or chlamydia regularly. These diseases can also affect people. Therefore, you need to be additionally careful.

The blood count and complete chemistry must be conducted just before the breeding season to make sure that the birds do not have any infections or other health issues.

Venipuncture should be carried out on the birds regularly. While the vein is easily available, you need to be careful about he kicks that the bird will render during this test.

You can take blood samples of your birds with the help of cannulated wings.

You need to check the birds for coccidiosis. You will also have to make sure that coccidiocide is administered to the birds from a very young age. Make sure that you follow the instructions of the manufacturer while using this product as it may lead to intestinal problems in the birds.

These routine tests need to be carried out by a vet. In case of large birds like the Emu, it is good to find a vet who can come to your facility for monthly and annual checkups instead of the other way around.

If you are a new Emu owner, the whole process of learning to capture and handle the bird will take a lot of time. In the meantime, the vet will have to visit your facility.

In any case, a bird as large as the Emu can cause a lot of commotion and fear among the other animals and birds at the vet. If startled, these birds can attack and cause serious injuries to other people and their pets. So, the best idea would be to look for a good vet who pays home visits. This makes it convenient for you and also reduces a lot of stress on your part.

3. Common health issues

There are some common health problems that Emus are susceptible to like any other species of birds. There are various options to prevent most of these conditions.

Some of these diseases may be contagious and may have a very low incubation period, which means that the bird may not show any symptoms at all but may become ill or even die of a certain disease overnight.

Careful examination of your bird and routine checkups will help you become alert to these health issues and will also make you more sensitive to the mild symptom.

The most common health issues with Emus are:

a. Heavy metal poisoning
This normally happens when the bird accidentally ingests any heavy metal such as Zinc or lead.

Symptoms:

Regurgitation of water
Persistent thirst
Listlessness
Vomiting
Depression
Weakness
Depression
Loss of motor control and coordination
Seizures
Liver and renal issues
Reddish droppings and urates
Lack of appetite.
Bright green droppings

Diagnosis:
The vet will look for any radiographic evidence of the metal that has been ingested by the bird.

Response to parenteral fluids and treatment with Calcium EDTA is seen as a form of diagnosis.

The zinc and lead concentration in the blood is noted down.

Treatment
Organic compounds called chelates are used to treat any heavy metal toxicity. These compounds are known to detoxify any metal agent.

They are injected into the body continuously directly to the muscles till the levels of the metal in the body reach the normal levels.

Prevention:
Any heavy metal scrap in the enclosure should be cleared out. This includes material used for fencing.

Old paint and soldering can contain lead. Therefore, it is necessary to keep the enclosure free from both these substances.

b. Obstruction of the GI tract
The gastrointestinal tract may become obstructed if the bird ingests large objects like nails or plastic parts from equipment and machinery.

Symptoms:

Gasping
Regurgitation
Choking
A lump in the throat due to the object that is ingested.
Abnormal sounds
Lack of appetite
Lethargy
Depression
Weakness
Swallowing continuously

Diagnosis:
You will need a complete radiography of the Gastro Intestinal tract to determine the object that is stuck and the location of the object.

Endoscopy can also determine the area where the object is stuck.

Examination by touch or palpation is also applicable in most cases.

Treatment:
In most cases, surgical processes are required to remove these objects. The bird is sedated with a very mild dose of anesthesia for this procedure.

Prevention:
All the nails that have been used in the enclosure should be nailed tightly into place.

Examine the enclosure on a regular basis to make sure that there are no sharp or large objects lying around that may be ingested by the bird.

c. Fractures of the leg or the wing
There are several instances when your bird may end up with a broken wing or leg. This needs to be properly examined and treated as your bird will have a lot of difficultly with mobility and may even show signs of aggression.

Causes:

Kicking fences
Fights between Emus
Legs or wings getting stuck in the fences
Improper handling methods
Improper transport of the birds
Unsafe designs of the enclosure

Symptoms of leg fractures:
Improper gait
Inability to stand properly
When the bird is trying to get up, he tends to scramble a lot in case of fractures.
Loss of balance and falling over.

You cannot really make out if the bird has fractured a leg when he is seated. They tend to sit normally. Only in case of extreme fractures when the leg looks twisted does it show in a seated position.

Symptoms of wing fracture:
The wing hangs from the body in an abnormal fashion.
Weakness
Lack of appetite
Listlessness
Depression

The last three symptoms may even be seen in case of leg fractures.

Diagnosis:
X rays are used to determine the location of the fracture.
In some cases, ultrasound may also be used.

Treatment:
Slings can be used on Emus, as they are able to tolerate them for long periods.

In case the quality of the bone is normal, you may also use a plate to help the bird heal.

In case there is a fracture in the phalanges or the metatarsals, the joints are stabilized using casts made of fiberglass.

Wing fractures may not need any intervention at all if it is not a compound one.

Surgical procedures may be required in the case of leg fractures. However, these surgeries are almost always unsuccessful because management of your Emu post-surgery becomes quite a hassle.

Leg fractures in Emus are usually very serious and it may require euthanisation of the bird in most cases. This is in fact more humane than allowing the bird to suffer.

Prevention
Be very cautious when you are handling the bird.

If you notice that two birds are constantly fighting with one another, make sure you separate them.
The enclosure should be Emu friendly. This means that there should be no obstructions, holes in the ground or objects that can cause falls and injuries.

When you are holding the wings to restrain the bird, especially in the standing restraint, do not be persistent if the bird is struggling too much. This can lead to unwanted injuries, including fractures.

d. Skin Lacerations

There are several reasons why skin lacerations may be caused in birds. These lacerations in the skin can be very painful for the bird and can be really difficult for you to handle.

Causes:

Scraping against protruding sharp objects.
Getting caught in the fence.
Getting entangled with metal wires or even rough surfaced ropes.
Fighting with the other Emus in a group.

Symptoms:
Blood running from the laceration is the first and most obvious sign.

You may find dried blood around the laceration.

Several flies will congregate in the area that has been affected or is bleeding.

Lameness if the wound is on the leg or the pelvic area.

Depression if the wound is deep and painful.

Listlessness.

Treatment
You must never use flour or styptic pencils on wounds that are seen on the skin of the bird.

Cleanse the area with 3% hydrogen peroxide. You may need some assistance to restrain the bird while you do this.

Apply some pressure on the wound till the bleeding stops.

In case the laceration is ¼ of an inch or lesser, cleaning with hydrogen peroxide is good enough to manage it.

If the laceration is bigger than ¼ of an inch, it may need a suture that can be provided by an Avian vet.

Common methods used to close the wound include sutures and staples without any local anesthesia in most cases.

First aid ointments or any topical ointment should never be administered to your bird without consulting your vet first. There are chances of permanent damage to the feathers. In some cases, the wounds may lead to secondary health problems and side effects.

Antiseptic powders may be applied when the wound is healing. This can be applied on the wound only when a vet recommends it.

You will also need a spray that can deter flies. Make sure that this spray does not harm the bird or irritate the wound.

Prevention:
Inspect the enclosure of your Emu on a regular basis.

Any sharp or pointed object must be removed.

You also need to take care that there are no sharp objects on the floor of the enclosure as it may get into the foot of the bird.

Wires should never stick out of the fencing area.

If you notice aggression among birds, separate them immediately.

e. Endoparasitic infections

There are several parasites that can enter the system of your Emu and make use of the bird's body as a host. This in turn causes several health issues that need to be taken care of in order to prevent the spreading of these diseases within the flock. In some serious cases of infection, death may occur without any prior sign or symptom.

Causes:
Nematoades or Roundworms
Trematodes or flukes
Cestodes or tapeworms

Symptoms:
Lack of appetite
Diarrhea
Anorexia
Pneumonia
Excessive hunger
Difficulty in breathing

Anemia
Neoplasia
Hepatitis

Diagnosis
Fecal examinations
Fecal flotation and smears
Looking for the presence of eggs in feces or regurgitated matter.

Treatment
Anthelmintic treatment
Proper nutrition
Supplementation

Prevention
Get regular fecal examinations of your bird done to look for the parasitic load in your flock of Emus.

Make sure you engage in regular worming of the birds.
Regular cleaning of the enclosure reduces parasitic load.

Make sure that feces is removed from the ground every day.

Use anti spill feeders.

Provide clean drinking water.

Keep the water container at a certain height to make sure that birds do not sit in the water or stamp around in it.

f. Ectoparasites
Ectoparasites are found on the skin of the bird and are usually the result of improper husbandry practices.

Causes:

Flies
Mites
Ticks
Lice

Symptoms:
Feather loss
Excessive itching

Visible ectoparasites
Lack of appetite
Anemia in case of tick infestation

Treatment
You can use sprays and powders of mites, lice and flies
Ticks require manual removal

Prevention
You need to keep ticks, flies and mites away with proper physical examinations of the bird.

You may take preventive measures such as administering the powders and removing visible ticks regularly.

g. Bacterial Infections
In case there is overcrowding in the enclosure, infections by bacteria is very common. There are some strains of bacteria that can be transmitted from one bird to the other causing serious infections within the flock.

Causes:

E.Coli bacteria
Salmonella
Mycoplasma
Mycobacterium avium
Clostridium perfringens
Poor nutrition
Poor hygiene
High stress

Symptoms:
Weakness
Diarrhea
Lethargy
Vomiting
Lack of appetite
Sudden death
Depression
Sinusitis
Pneumonia
Inflammation of air sacs
Inflammation of the stomach

Inflammation of the umbilical cord stump in hatchlings
Bacterial strains in the blood stream
Lameness and swollen joints

Diagnosis:
Fecal analysis
Blood tests
Radiographs

Treatment:
In some cases, antibiotics may work on the infected birds. Unfortunately, most bacterial infections do not have any proper treatment and it is very important for you to focus on the preventive measures.

Prevention
Clean the feces daily
Remove any dirt and debris
Do not overcrowd the enclosures
Disinfect and clean the enclosures regularly.
Isolate birds with infections to prevent the disease from spreading.

h. Chlamydophilosis

This is a serious infection for Emu birds. In fact, this condition is never really treatable and a bird that is affected will always remain a carrier of the condition.

Causes:

Infection by *Chlamydophila*

Symptoms:

Conjunctivitis
Nasal discharge
Moist respiratory noises
Watery eyes
Coughing
Sneezing
Green pigments in the urine or biliverdinuria
Lethargy
Sudden weight loss
Lethargy

Diagnosis:

71

Fecal testing
Swab of the cloaca and the choana for a Polymerase Chain Reaction.
Clearview test of the swabs mentioned above.
Blood test using an Immunocomb blood test kit.
Treatment:
Injections of doxycycline for seven weeks, once each week.

Oral medicines can be administered through the food or water for a month.

Prevention:
Quarantine any new bird that is included in the flock.

Birds that are infected should be isolated at the earliest.

Disinfecting the enclosure on a regular basis is a must. You can use agents like hydrogen peroxide, bleach and alcohol to disinfect the enclosure.

Make sure that your birds are not too stressed.

i. Aspergillosis
This is a fungal disorder that affects most birds. It is usually the result of improper animal husbandry.

Causes:

Fungus called aspergilla is responsible for the condition.
Wet areas on the hay
Contamination of the feed
Bacterial infection
Over use of antibiotics
Immunosuppression

Symptoms:
Wheezing
Coughing
Choking
Wheezing
Weakness
Depression

Diagnostic tests

It is necessary to isolate the organism that is present in the lesions through a microbial culture.

Analysis of any signs of leucocystosis.

Endoscopic examinations to study the fungal plaques in the trachea, the lungs and air sacs.

Cystologic examination of the discharge in the eyes or nose.

Serology helps detect this condition quite easily.

Radiographs are necessary to check for any multifocal densities inside the lungs, the air sacs or trachea. These densities represent the fungal plaque.

Treatment
Lesions that are easily accessible will be removed through surgical methods.

Antifungal drugs can be provided orally or through injections.

Nebulizers are prescribed in some cases.

Supplemental heat should be provided.

Tube feeding is necessary in case of birds that show signs of appetite loss.

Oxygen supplementation may become necessary in extreme conditions.

Prevention
Follow strict standards of hygiene within the enclosure.

The bedding material should be clean and dry.

Straw, hay and other agricultural products should be refrained from use as a bedding material.
The feed should be stored properly.
Always check the feed for any signs of fungal growth.

The hay you give your birds should be free from any mold.

Preventive anti-fungal medication may be provided to the birds.

j. Candidiasis
This is yet another common infection among birds that renders them very weak and depressed.

Cause:

Infection by the yeast *Candida albicans.*

Symptoms:
Depression
Inability to assimilate nutrients from the food that they consume.
Ruffled feathers
Scabs, plaques and whitish ulcers near the joint of the upper and lower beak
Bad breath
Thickened areas on near the mouth and beak, filled with mucus.
Erosion of the ventriculus lining
Weight loss
Vomiting
Diarrhea
Nasal discharge
Change in the voice of the bird
Inability to breathe
Rapid breathing
Inability to carry out physical activities

Diagnosis
Smears from the crop, feces and the oral cavity are examined with gram stains.

Treatment
Antifungal medicines are administered
In case of oral and skin infections, topical ointments containing amphotericin B can be applied.

Elimination of any risk factors.

Prevention
When any negative factor affecting the bird is present in the enclosure, the bird becomes susceptible to this infection.

The enclosure should be clean.

Proper nutrition must be provided to the bird at all times.

Prevent contact with birds that are potentially unwell.

Eliminate any cause of stress in the bird.

Add nystatin to the formula used for hatchlings that are hand raised.

In case of birds that have been on antibacterial medicines for a long time, you may administer a few antifungal medicines.

Never re-use the leftovers of one hand fed chick on another bird.

Items used to nurse young chicks should always be disinfected before putting them back.

k. Protozal diseases
The most common protozoal disease among Emus in coccidiosis which is caused by an infection by Eimeria.

Symptoms:

Lethargy
Listlessness
Blood on the body or in the droppings
Sudden weight loss
Diarrhea
Dehydration
Sudden death

Diagnosis
Laboratory examination is necessary to establish the condition.

Intestinal smears are examined to check for the growth and colonization of the protozoa.

These protozoans are identified based on the size, location and the shape of the protozoan.

Treatment
An anticoccidial drug such as toltrazuril or Baycox should be administered as soon as the condition has been diagnosed.

While administering any drug, you need to ensure that you follow all the instructions provided by the manufacturer.

The best way to administer these drugs is through drinking water.

Preventive measures:
Get your bird vaccinated. There are some effective vaccines that can be given to the bird when they are younger.

Moisture should not be present as coccidian thrive in the presence of moist conditions.

Make sure that the enclosure is fully dry and clean.

Ventilation in the enclosure is a must.

The enclosure should never be overcrowded.

You must try to build your enclosure on a dry well, a sandy and sunny yard that is north facing.

The birds may develop immunity to one strain of coccidia but it does not protect them from the condition entirely.

Try to provide vaccinations through the drinking water on a regular basis to keep your birds fully protected at all times.

l. Reproductive problems
It is common for most captive birds to have reproductive disorders if they are not given the right nutrition and care when the eggs are being formed.

The most common types of reproductive diseases include oviductal infection, ruptured oviduct, egg binding etc. Egg binding is one condition that all bird owners and breeders must be aware of. Although the causes are not really known, there are some speculations of what may lead to egg binding in hens.

Causes:

Genetic factors
Malnutrition
Inadequate area for nesting
Excessive egg laying
Obesity

Lack of exercise
Inadequate intake of calcium during the breeding season.

Symptoms:
Too much movement in the cloacal region near the ventrodorsal area of the bird while it is running is a sign of some reproductive issue.

Vaginal prolapse is an indication of reproductive issues in the hen

Swelling in the pericloacal area that is too large is a sign of hernias in the peritoneal region.
Depression
Lack of appetite
Constant sitting
Weakness
Weight loss
Depression

Diagnosis:
Study of the blood samples
Biochemistry of the serum
Study of the oviduct cultures
Radiology
Ultrasonography
Abdominocentesis
Physical examination
Palpation of the cloacal region
Study of the reproductive history of the hen
Eversion of the phallic area

Treatment:
Surgical procedures may help in some cases of egg binding
Lubrication relieves egg binding
Calcium injections need to be administered
Vitamin A, D, E and selenium supplementation is a must
Ambient temperature of the bird should be improved
Dextrose and fluids should be administered
The reproductive tract can be contracted to urge the bird to pass the egg out.
Oxytocin injections help to a large extent
Prostaglandin gel may be applied
If there is a visible obstruction, you must not apply any medication without consulting your vet

Prevention
Proper nutrition
Good management of the birds
Adequate exercise
Correct breeding techniques
Good hygiene practices

m. Environmental diseases

The fluctuations in temperature can affect the health of the bird to a large extent. The most important environmental factor is heat. If the bird does not have enough heat or if the heat is more than what is required by the bird's body, the result is usually adverse.

Hyperthermia means the elevation of the body temperature more than require. Hypothermia occurs when the temperature of the body is drastically reduced.

Causes of hyperthermia:

Inadequate shade and shelter
Too much chasing and stress during capture
Wrong restraining techniques
Transportation of the birds when the temperature outside is too high.

Cause for hypothermia
Advanced state of certain diseases
Inadequate heating facilities
Feather loss during cold weather due to improper nutrition

Symptoms of hyperthermia
Sudden increase in the rate of respiration
Weakness and fatigue
Panting
Sudden bouts of unconsciousness

Symptoms of hypothermia
Lethargy
Decreased heart rate
Weakness
The body becomes cold to touch

Treatment of hyperthermia:
Removing any heat source

Cooling the body of the Emu with fans or air conditioning
Seeking immediate veterinary assistance

Treating hypothermia
Warming the body of the bird with electric blankets
Wrapping the body with a large blanket
Increasing environmental temperature using a heater
Minimizing the loss of heat
Treating the underlying disease that is causing hypothermia
Prevention
Providing proper facilities in the housing areas
Heating and cooling facilities if you live in an area that has extreme weather conditions.
Ensure that your capture techniques are correct.

n. Nutritional diseases
Bad management is responsible for nutritional problems among birds. It is difficult for birds to obtain food on their own if their enclosure is not large enough with enough flora and fauna.

When you have limited options for food sources, you need to make sure that your bird gets everything that is required for proper development and growth. The most common nutritional disease that you notice in birds is vitamin deficiency.

Symptoms

Weakness
Poor condition of the body
Lethargy
Sudden weight loss
Stunted growth
Deformities
Failure to grow
Depression
Too much water consumption
Increased urination
Vulnerability to many diseases

Treatment:
Providing a well-balanced meal
Increasing the food intake in case of birds that are underweight
Providing vitamin supplements

Prevention
Ensure that the birds have enough space to move around.
They should be able to get ample sunlight
Consult a vet to help you with the nutritional plan for your bird.

When it comes to the health of your Emus, the most important thing that you need to focus on is preventive care. As long as you are able to take care of your husbandry practices and are able to provide the birds with the nutrition that they need, you should be able to keep most health problems at bay.

For anyone who is looking at bringing Emus home for the first time, you need to understand that the only things your bird will ever need are enough space to move around, food and a clean environment.

Of course, regular vet checkups are a must. You need to make sure that your vet will be able to travel to your home or farm to examine the birds. The thing with Emus is that they are really hard to transport. Unless it is an emergency, the process of capturing and transporting the bird adds to the stress and may alleviate the health issues that the bird is already suffering from.

4. Quarantining Measures

Whenever you introduce new birds to a flock, quarantining is a must. This gives you the chance to observe the new bird for any signs of illnesses that may harm the rest of the flock.

You see, in most cases, the incubation period of any disease is about 90 days. Until then, your bird may not have the slightest sign of a disease. However, you can never be sure whether a certain bird is a carrier of a disease or not. So quarantining is necessary.

There are some right practices that you will have to follow in order to quarantine the birds properly. Quarantining is also necessary when an illness is seen in a bird in the flock. The bird must instantly be moved to a designated area for quarantine.

The area that you choose for quarantining should ensure that the new bird or the sick bird is away for all the other animals, including pets and other farm animals.

You can choose a small paddock that is away from the rest of the enclosures. If you have people visiting your farm, you also need to make sure that the bird is kept away from them. Diseases like salmonellosis and chlamydia can be transferred from the bird to people.

You need to keep the area of quarantine as quiet as possible. It should be free from any form of stress. There should be adequate warmth, shelter and space in this area. You also need to make it easily accessible in case of an emergency with respect to the bird.

Here are a few quarantining guidelines that can help you with your Emu:

The new bird or the sick bird should be quarantined for at least 30 days.

The bird must be supervised by a vet during this period.

If the bird has received any treatment, you will have to continue to monitor it even after the bird shows complete recovery.

The vet should give you consent to let the bird into the same enclosure as the other birds.

In this quarantining period, in case one of the birds shows signs of an infectious disease, you will have to isolate it immediately.
Following the detection of a disease in a new bird, whole group should be quarantined one after the other to make sure that there are no carriers in the group.

If there is specific disease that you are concerned about, you need to make sure that the quarantining period matches with the incubation period of the disease in question.

The person who is taking care of the birds should never work with other animals or birds who belong to the same group taxonomically. In case this is not an option, you need to carry out feeding, cleaning and other activities last with the quarantined bird.

The equipment required for feeding and cleaning should be maintained separately for the bird that is being quarantined. The quarantined equipment should be disinfected after use as much as possible.

Any soiled bedding or food of the quarantined bird should be disposed in such a way that it is not accessible by other animals or birds on the farm. The best way to do this is by burning these items.

You need to make sure that there are no exposures accidentally to other birds and animals. This means that you need to wear protective clothing, gloves and masks when you are handling the quarantined bird. It is also a good idea to have a foot bath with disinfectants. Make sure that you do not have any clothing on you that has been exposed to the quarantined bird. Also wash your hands carefully before handling the food and other items of the other birds.

After the quarantining period is over, conduct a full physical examination of the bird in question before you actually release the bird into the enclosure of the other birds. You need to look for ticks or any exotic seeds that may be hidden in the feathers of the new bird.

All these quarantining measures should be taken when you are introducing a mate to your birds as well. The more precautions you take, the healthier your flock will be.

5. Finding a vet for your Emu

The vet that you need to associate with for your Emu is quite different from the vets you would go to for other pets. Emu vets should be well versed in avian medicine and must also understand the requirements of large farm animals, since most communal groups of Emus function just like livestock. So, your vet also functions almost like a veterinarian for livestock.

Here are a few things that you must look for in a vet for your Emu:

They should have the ability to treat birds. An avian vet specializes in treating birds and would have spent a majority of their practice hours on birds and exotic pets.

You can even look for a vet who can treat exotic pets. These individuals are adept in treating birds and animals that have been imported or are native to an entirely different kind of setting in terms of their origins and environmental preferences.

There are several livestock experts in every country who may also have good understanding of Emus. You may contact these experts to know more about the avian vets in your locality.

The Internet is one of the best places to look for a veterinarian facility that suits your needs. You can search for recommended vets on the official website of the Association of Avian vets for the best results. You can even look for these vets on popular search engines.

Recommendations from other Emu farms or Emu owners in your town or city can help you the most. These recommendations come from people who have had their own pets examined by these vets. They will be able to give you the best perspective on the facilities and the specializations.

You can speak to vets who treat other domestic animals or pets. They will be able to recommend someone who can take best care of your Emus for you.

Once you have found a vet who is easily accessible and has the experience to treat a bird like the Emu, you need to visit the facility to make sure that your bird is in good hands. You must ask the following questions to your vet:

Will they be able to treat your Emus in your home or on the farm?

How many times in a month will they be able to devote to these visits?

How will they be able to handle emergencies, if any?

In case there are any surgical requirements, will they be able to provide any in-patient facilities for the bird?

How do they keep themselves updated about the requirements of birds like Emus that have become domestic choices relatively recently?

If these questions are answered satisfactorily, you can leave your Emus under the care of the vet. Make sure that you look for a vet well in advance or even before you bring your Emu home. You do not want to have an emergency and then scramble through your contacts to look for a suitable vet.

Chapter 7: Emu Behavior

Understanding Emu behavior is the key to making sure that you are providing your birds with all the facilities that the birds require in order to thrive and function to their best ability.

1. Behavior aspects of Emus

There are several aspects of Emu behavior that you will have to know about in order to bond with them and really make these pets feel welcome in your home:

a. Activity

These birds are diurnal in nature. This means that they are more active during the day. They need to rest and sleep at night. In the wild, these birds are nomadic in nature. They actually follow the rains in order to find their food.

If Emus are chased by predators, they can run at close to 50km per hour. Normally, the bird can cover up to 7km every hour. With each stride being 9 feet in length, this does not come as a surprise. Emus, during the season of migration or movement, tend to walk for close to 1000kms to find their food. They cover more than 25kms every day.

In the months of summer and spring, Emus begin to double their body weight. This is when they are preparing to breed and the birds need to increase their food consumption to about 4 kilos every day.

When the breeding season actually begins they will reduce the food consumption to almost 100g every day! These birds will spend a lot of time foraging and looking around for food. This really depends upon the season and their requirements.

During the day, Emus are busy feeding, running, playing, swimming and just wandering. These birds are very inquisitive by nature and it is quite endearing to watch how the simplest of things will grab their attention in no time.

b. Social behavior

These birds are normally solitary creatures even though they are usually seen in large flocks. They just prefer to keep themselves busy and will do their own thing while sticking by the flock that they have chosen.

Usually, these birds will move in flocks in search of food and resting areas. Many people do not consider these birds too social and believe that they only depend upon the group to fulfill their own needs.

In the countryside, you will normally see these birds in pairs. Their homes can extend to up to 30 square kilometers. Of course, they will be possessive about certain areas in this wide expanse of land. They will, however, try their best to avoid another bird. In case of any confrontation, the leg is the weapon of choice for most of these birds.

A brood tends to stay together after the male abandons the nest. Then eventually this group will break up and the birds will wander off alone or in pairs.

Emus have certain specific calling patterns. There are two calls that are very common: the drum and the grunt. The grunt is usually used be the male in order to provide a warning. The drum is the more serious sign of aggression.

Females use the drum a courting call. They also claim their territory using the boom. In order to make these typical calls, the Emus make use of the tracheal pouch that provides a chamber of resonance. This low frequency call can be carried to about 1km.

Displays with calls are common. Emus normally fluff out all the feathers near the neck and will produce this characteristic drumming sound. They will also stretch themselves up and show off their personality with a lot of vigor.

In case of the chicks, piping calls are seen until the birds are about 5 months old. This is when the voice breaks in the chicks. A small opening is formed in the trachea to aid communication using the air sacs.

Usually, Emus are extremely tolerant birds. They will show aggression in some parts of the year. Females tend to be a lot more aggressive than the males, however. When the males are broody, they become very aggressive too. They may even show signs of aggression against their own partner.

c. Bathing
Emus love to bathe! These birds are natural born swimmers. They do not use the wings to swim or splash the water. Instead, these birds tend to flop into the water and just roll around till the feathers are wet. This is very amusing to the beholder as the bird tend to look really uncomfortable splashing and jumping in the water. When they come out of the water, they shake it off of the feathers just as dogs do.

In case you are unable to provide your bird with creeks and dams to swim in, you can also have sprinklers installed. The birds will really enjoy this and it also becomes part of behavior enhancement for the birds.

2. Behavioral problems in Emus

In most cases, Emus are quite well behaved. That is why most national parks and zoos across the world consider it quite safe to have these birds walk around without any harness.

However, once these birds get accustomed to people, they tend to display overconfidence in their presence. This makes them become quite a hassle if people are carrying food or are even wearing shiny clothes or jewelry. Their inquisitive approach can scare children quite a bit. One good thing about the Emus is that their pecking does not really cause any damage. However, it can lead to a lot of stress for a person who is experiencing it for the first time.

When these birds are being hand fed, especially in zoos and national parks, they may peck at people in an attempt to reach out to the food. Emus that roam freely will also try to steal food and will also be able to understand the packaging of the food in order to open it and eat out of it.

In general, Emus are easy birds to be around. They never really intend any harm and are highly docile creatures. They may, however, even become aggressive to the person whom they interact with the most when the breeding season begins. As a safety measure, it is recommended that you have a helper with you in case you have to deal with multiple birds at one time.

a. Signs of stress

You may notice sudden feather loss in Emus along with attempts to escape from your home or farm. This usually means that your bird is undergoing some form of stress. The common symptoms of stress are:

Moodiness
Irritability
Depression
Feather picking
Increased aggression
Excessive physical activity
Increase in elimination of wastes
Less interest in socialization
Abnormality in the vocalization

Emus are generally very relaxed by nature. If they are startled or caught off guard, they will become highly defensive.

b. enrichment

For birds as curious as the Emu, providing behavior enrichment is quite an easy task. They will be interested in just about anything novel and shiny! Some ideas for behavior enrichment of your Emus include:

Tying sticks with rags and dangling them over the fence of the enclosure

Hanging up shiny objects like disco balls on the trees

Filling up a large 2L bottle with marbles and an assortment of objects that shine. You can close this bottle tight and just give it to your bird as a toy.

Providing sprinklers or simple water hoses. You can even include man made ponds or waterfalls in the enclosure.

Adding inflatable toys in the ponds.

Hiding food items all across the enclosure including the branches of the trees or the top of the fence.

This really helps engage the birds to the fullest and prevents any chances of behavioral problems due to inactivity and boredom.

3. The Emu and other birds or animals

Your Emu will be very pleasant to introduce to people or pets in most cases. However, these birds can be really unpredictable. So, any introduction within the flock or to new people and pets should be done quite cautiously.

If you are introducing your Emu to a flock, the first thing you will have to do is quarantine the bird. You will have to make the release of the bird into the flock very slowly and easily.

Once the birds have been quarantined, you need to keep the new bird in the holding area for a while. This makes the flock aware of the fact that there is another bird in the vicinity. You may notice a rather unpleasant initial reaction and even some aggressive behavior initially. Unless the birds harm each other, there is no need to pull the new bird away. All you need to do is ensure that the bird is well monitored.

When you know that the birds are going to get along well, you can just leave the new birds alone. Introductions and reintroductions are fairly easy with Emus. As mentioned before, these birds just like to mind their own business and will just not interfere.

a. Intraspecific compatibility

You will notice with these birds that intraspecific compatibility is not really that difficult. Intraspecific compatibility refers to the compatibility of birds and animals of the same species. Here are a few things you will notice in the case of the Emu:

You can easily house males and females together.

Large groups of Emus can be housed together easily as long as each bird has enough space for himself.
The space that you give your Emus should be large enough to allow the birds to ignore one another when required.

Removing females from the enclosure may become necessary when the males begin to incubate the eggs. This is because the males become extremely aggressive when they are in this stage.

b. Interspecific compatibility

Interspecific compatibility refers to the compatibility between animals and birds from different species. This is very important information if you already have a farm with livestock or have other pets in your loving little home. Here are some tips to ensure that both animals are safe:

You may house Emus with birds that have the same temperament. Both the creatures need to be docile in order to get along with one another.

It is best to house macropods and Emus together. This includes kangaroos and koalas. The reason for this is that these creatures are extremely non-threatening and quite placid, too.

On free-range farms, you may have goats, sheep, ducks and even chickens on the same farm. These animals will rarely get in each other's way.

If your Emu has been housed separately for several years on end, it is quite natural for him to get a little territorial in nature. Several farms and zoos can tell you by experience that it is in fact true.

If you introduce an animal from a separate species to an old flock of Emus, they will all surround the new animal and just tower over him. This itself can be quite intimidating to the new creature.

In some cases, the whole flock tends to corner the new animal and will begin to stomp if they feel threatened. That is why it is absolutely necessary to monitor your Emus and also other animals that have been introduced into their enclosure.

In case the new animal or bird survives the curiosity of these birds, they will just lose interest eventually and will leave him alone. If you practice slow release with the help of a holding enclosure, it may become a lot easier for the two species to really interact and get accustomed to one another.

One thing you need to be very careful about is hygiene when you are housing animals and birds from different species. There is always a good chance of infection spreading from one species to the other. This can become quite hard to handle as the disease will affect each species differently and it will be up to you to take care of them. Instead it is a good idea to have separate feeding and drinking enclosures along with routine cleaning activities like turning the substrate and removing fecal matter.

c. Susceptibility to captivity

Emus are quite accustomed to being raised in captivity. They are seen in several wildlife parks and zoos across the globe. These birds are very easy to care for and will need lesser resources in comparison to other farm animals and even pets. They are quite the interesting creatures that are really fun to be around.

These birds only thrive for about 15 years in the wild and can live up to 35 years in captivity. That shows how comfortable these birds have become to a domestic set up over the years. They are also very entertaining pets to own.

Chapter 8: Breeding Emus

Most people bring home Emus with the intention of breeding them. These birds have a rather unique mating system that can be very interesting to study and understand. If you are bringing a bird home with the main intention of breeding them, you will have to have them sexed by a veterinarian first as the male and the female look almost identical.

If you are buying from a reputed breeder, he should be able to help you with this as well. Nevertheless, seek assistance from a vet to be doubly sure.

1. The mating system

In the case of Emus, the females are the dominant ones during the breeding and mating phase. The females are polygamous. This means that in one breeding season, they may have multiple partners after mating with their primary breeding partner.

This system of mating or breeding is known as sequential or successive polyandry. After the birds have been paired, they will stick to their partners for at least 5 months. This normally happens in the summer.

The female, as we mentioned, dominates this pairing and is the one to initiate courtship. The male tends to be aggressive when the incubation period begins. Interestingly, the females have no part in the incubation of the eggs. The male, in this stage, is also aggressive towards the female he pairs up with.

The female does not provide any care for the hatchlings either. This too is taken care of by the male birds.

The Emu mating phase is completed in four phases:

Courtship
Mounting
Intromission followed by Ejaculation
Postcoital display

a. Courtship

It is the female who generally initiates the courtship with the production of a booming sound. This sound travels to almost 1km. Then, the female will fluff her feathers and display typical behavior such as bobbing, grunting, ducking and dipping.

The males may show some aggression towards one another. They will normally chase each other around and will drive the other contenders away with powerful kicks.

A strong bond is formed between one of the contending males and the female in heat. To show this bonding, the birds will raise their heads and will just walk around one another. Following this the male will put his head on the female's back and head. He will touch her with his chest and will push forward.

The female will walk for a few minutes with the male and will crouch down to let him mount her.

b. Mounting

The male Emu will sit right behind the female Emu almost at a right angle. He will slowly advance towards her tail. Following this, he places his legs on either side of the female and will take a seated position behind her.

After this the phallus is partially evaginated. The mail will then bring the phallus to the cloaca of the female, just touching it. When the female feels this she will lower her neck and push her abdomen back toward the male, fully everting the cloaca to allow penetration.

c. Intromission followed by Ejaculation

The male moves closer to the female and raises his body. This is when the intromission occurs and the phallus of the bird becomes erect. The male will grab the neck of the female during the ejaculation

d. Postcoital display

After the ejaculation, the male will dismount. As he stands, he fluffs all his feathers. The penis is withdrawn into the body. The male then preens himself and moves away from the female.

Then there are a few signs that he displays to show nesting behavior. He will lower his head till it is just above the ground. Then, he makes some grunting noises. The most common nesting behavior is picking up of leaves and grass and replacing them like a nest.

The female Emu will not stand during this display. After it is complete, she stands up while keeping her body fully erect and higher than the normal standing height.

This marks the end of the coital period and you can wait for the bird to lay the eggs following this rather interesting display. The female may display courting and may even mate with more partners after the primary partner as mentioned before. Even these mating behaviors are the same as the ones mentioned above. It is easy to identify a female in heat and the whole courtship phase after a few breeding seasons.

If you have several birds in your enclosure, they will find their own mates. The courting will determine which female mates with which male. It is recommended that you have an equal number of males and females in the group.

However, if you have two or three Emus in your backyard, it is best to have one male and one female. In any case the numbers of the females per male may be higher but not the other way around.

2. Breeding in captivity

Emus are fairly easy to breed in captivity. These birds will mate readily if the daylight hours are reduced as per their requirements. When the daylight hours reduce, it has been noticed that they will reduce their food consumption drastically and will have a surge of breeding hormones.

Just before the breeding season begins, adult Emus that are in decent reproductive condition will double their body weight. A layer of fat is deposited between the muscle groups of these birds and the gut cavity. If the birds are in good reproductive condition, they will also showcase the breeding behavior mentioned above.

The feathers of the female become black and thick just before the breeding season begins. She will have black feathers on her neck and head. The plumes on the body tend to become darker. This is a sign that she is willing to take a mate. She will also start making distinct rattling noises.

As for the males, they become extremely hormonal before the breeding season. The testosterone levels and the luteinizing hormones increase. The testicles of the Emus will double in size during this period.

Males begin to eat less and focus all their time and energy on constructing a nest for the female.

Emus breed seasonally. Pairing usually begins during January or December. In the month of April, breeding actually occurs. The eggs are usually laid around October or November. Chicks will hatch early June or even in December at times. The peak time for eggs to hatch is usually July and August.

The breeding age for Emus is normally when they are about 2 years of age. However, birds that hatch later in a season tend to breed later too. These birds will normally breed at the age of three.

In captivity, Emus will live up to the age of 30. They will continue to produce eggs till they are about 16 years old.

You can expect your Emus to breed year after year after they have reached the right age. In fact, when the season is good enough, the females even have the ability to lay more than one clutch of eggs, often going up to three clutches.

The Emu nests, as we have seen, are made by the male Emus. They make use of leaves, grass, barks and sticks to build these nests. If you have an enclosure for your birds, you have to make sure that this nesting material is available for the birds. You can even add the nesting material into the enclosure after the birds have reached the breeding season.

Emus need to have secluded and protected nests. For this reason, you need to make sure that rocks, trees and shrubs are available for the birds to put their nests under. If these barriers and proper nesting materials are not available, there can be serious issues like improper breeding behavior and even egg binding.

3. Diet for a breeding bird

Your Emu will begin to eat excessively when the breeding season begins.

You need to make sure that fat gain is limited in females till they reach breeding age. This is until they are about 12 months old. You can increase the reproductive fitness of your birds by following these simple methods.

This means that you will have to provide the bird with a unrestricted access to the foods that you normally feed them. In addition to this you need to supplement the meals with hay, pasture and Lucerne pellets.

A breeder meal should contain the following. The quantity represents the percentage of the meal that should contain this food group:

Wheat: 30%
Sorghum: 31.6%
Bone and meat meal: 10.3%
Soya bean meal: 4.9%
Sunflower meal: 6.5%
Millrun: 10%
Limestone: 5.7%

Salt: 0.22%
DL methionine: 0.17%
L Lysine HCL 0.07%
Mineral and vitamin mix: 0.5%

Any supplementation that you give the bird should be done only after you consult the vet. As your females approach the egg laying season, you will have to provide the above mentioned diet which will give them all the nutrition required. This proportion of the food items will help the bird in proper formation of the eggs.

You need to provide this diet to the birds at least six weeks before the actual breeding season begins. This is because the egg formation takes approximately five weeks to develop.
You also need to make sure that the male Emus have access to this diet. This makes them more fertile and ensures that they have enough reserves for in their bodies before incubation begins.

4. The incubation period

A female lays about 6 to 14 eggs in each clutch. The eggs are large and dark green in color. The average size of the egg is 130mmX90mm. They normally weight about 500-700 grams each.

The females lay the eggs very slowly. Normally, the time between the laying of the first egg and the next is can be several days long. The rate of laying eggs increases with each egg that is laid and is fastest towards the end of the clutch.

The clutch size can be higher in some cases. It can go up to a maximum of 25 eggs. This occurs when the female has mated with several other males. She will lay all the fertilized eggs in a single nest.

Even after the first clutch has been laid, the female may continue to mate. This leads to multiple clutches in one breeding season.

The eggs are incubated by the male for a total of eight weeks. During this time the male bird does not even leave the nest. The bird stays in the nest and does not move to drink, eat or even relieve himself.

The necks of the male rest on the ground and the body temperature drops by about 4 degrees. The only time the male stands is when the eggs need to be turned. This is done about 10 times every day.

During this time, the male Emu survives on the body fat that he put on before the breeding season started. They also consume the morning dew that is easy to access from the nest. One third of the male's body weight is lost during the incubation period.

Male Emus may also adopt chicks that are lost or abandoned if the chicks are of the same age as his own.

5. Fledging

Once the chicks have hatched, you will notice that they are rather active and energetic. They will be ready to leave the nest when they are about three days old.

Male Emus are responsible for raising the chicks. Until the chicks are about 18 months old, they are under the care of the parent bird. You may choose to pull the birds away as soon as the eggs have hatched.

Unlike most baby birds, Emu chicks are quite developed from the time they are born. They can walk around properly and can even feed themselves from the time they are born.

The maximum development is seen up to the age of 11 weeks in case of Emus. You need to take note of the average height and weight of the chicks over the weeks. All the height measurements are taken when the birds are in a complete upright position while the necks are extended completely. On an average, the weight of the bird as it develops is:

Hatch: 400g
3 months: 8kg
6 months: 19kg
1 year: 30 kg
2 years: 50 kg

You can determine the rate of development and the health of the birds with good record keeping. You should make sure that you note the hatch dates to keep a progressive check on the birds.

6. Artificial incubation

In some cases, you may want to incubate the eggs yourself. This is a common practice in most commercial Emu farms. There may be other problems like the male getting affected by a disease, death of the male or even abandonment of a brood.

a. Type of incubator

There are incubators that are specific to Emu eggs. You can even have regular poultry incubators customized to hold the eggs of your Emu. The results are usually as good as Emu specific incubators.

The incubators that are designed for Emu eggs are usually able to hold about 3 turning racks or hatching racks. The eggs are rotated horizontally automatically. The eggs that have set will hatch in one cabinet. All the eggs will be secured properly to make sure that tumbling or walking does not occur.

These incubators will have high power fans that can keep the conditions within the incubator dry for the eggs to thrive well. There are certain standards that have been set in most countries for these incubators. These standards may vary and most good companies will comply with the standards and also make adjustments as required.

b. Temperature and humidity
The temperature of the incubators should be maintained at a constant of 35.25 degrees centigrade. The relative humidity should be set at about 45 to 50%. This standard needs to be maintained for the first 50 days of incubating the eggs.

Before the eggs are incubated, you need to make sure that they are collected on a daily basis. This reduces the chances of any problems pertaining to the pre-incubation stage. The eggs should then be disinfected properly. You may ask your vet to help you find a recognized process to sanitize the eggs.

After they have been collected, the eggs should be kept at temperatures between 10-15 degrees centigrade for about 10 days. The eggs that have just been removed from the cold storage area should be left out for about 18 hours till they reach room temperature.

When the eggs are being incubated, there are some standard procedures of hygiene that you need to follow. For instance, you need to avoid placing soiled eggs in the incubator. Make sure that the water of the incubator is changed on a daily basis. You will have to wash and fumigate each egg if possible in order to prevent any chances of bacterial infections within the group.

In case the incubator does not have a turning rack, you will have to make sure that you manually turn them at least 3 times each day. The turning should be done an odd number of times to make sure that the egg does not end up on the same side every night. This may cause the embryo to be stuck to one side of the shell.
After 47 days of incubation the eggs will normally pip and the baby Emus will hatch out. This is when you will have to transfer the newborn chicks to brooders. There are several different kinds of brooders that are available for you to choose from. Some people who are into backyard

raising and breeding will also opt for plain cardboard boxes as their brooders. These can be brought to the required temperature using gas heaters or infra-red lamps.

You need to maintain the following temperature standards on an average when you brood the chicks yourself:
1 to 7 days: 30 deg. Celsius and above
7 to 14 days: 28 deg. Celsius
14 to 21 days: 26 deg. Celsius
21 to 28 days: 24 deg. Celsius

It is very important to maintain these temperature standards to keep the birds comfortable. You will also notice certain signs that will tell you that your temperature conditions are probably not ideal. If the birds huddle together, you will have to increase the temperature and if the birds begin to move away from one another, it means that the temperature needs to be reduced.

c. Feeding
Chicks that are hand reared will need a specific diet to make sure that they thrive well and grow up properly. You will have to first teach the birds to peck at the eggs. You can use birds like chickens to teach the Emu chicks this skill. You can house two or three chicks with the hens to do this.

If this is not an option, you can be the one that teaches your baby birds. All you need to do is tap at the dish using a bright pen or stick. The inquisitive nature of the Emus will urge them to peck at the food that you are showing them.

During this time, you need to avoid any organic bedding that could be eaten by the chicks. You need to avoid grass or hay. The water dishes that you choose should be no more than 50mm in depth to ensure that the baby birds do not drown.

You can give your Emu chicks the following foods:

Turkey crumbles
Milled barley, wheat and corn

Mix these grains up and add 1 teaspoon of calcium, Lucerne meal and 1 tablespoon of fine gravel to every kilo of the mix that you give the bird. In case the Lucerne meal is unavailable, you can give the birds the same proportion of finely chopped green vegetables.

You need to make sure that you give your chicks dry food for the initial period. This makes them want to drink water. In fact, it is the dry food that helps these birds identify the fact that thirst is quenched by water.

With every week, you may increase the proportion of dry foods that you give your bird. By the time they are 8 weeks old, they should be eating at least 125 kilos of dry feed. You can give them free access to the food only after 12 weeks of age. Until then, restrict the access to 2 times a day.

Keep the water and feeding dishes clean. Wash them every day. You also need to disinfect the enclosure on a daily basis to prevent any bacterial or fungal development. Lastly, provide the same type of substrate every time you clean your bird's enclosure.

Conclusion

This book is the result of a lot of research with Emu farms and Emu owners. I hope that it has provided you with the required insight into the world of these amazing creatures.

On a concluding note, it is necessary for you to make sure that you can afford to give the Emu the time and money that it needs in order to thrive well. You also need to check for any licensing requirements in your state. Normally, these birds do not need any permit unless they have been brought to your facility for rehabilitation.

In any case, you will have to check with the wildlife department of your state in order to understand if you need to get any license as per the laws governing Emu breeding and rearing. You may even contact national parks and reserves for this information.

Once you are certain that you can bring an Emu home, continue to read up about the birds and learn more about the new techniques of rearing these birds. The more knowledgeable you are, the better birds you will raise.

References

It is good to keep your bank of knowledge updated. There are some websites and bird forums that will help you learn more about Emus and will provide you with great information.

Note: at the time of printing, all the websites below were working. As the internet changes rapidly, some sites might no longer live when you read this book. That is, of course, out of our control.

www.nswfmpa.org

http://www.exoticpetvet.net/

http://www.abc.net.au/

http://www.newworldencyclopedia.org/

http://www.hobbyfarms.com/

http://www.agmrc.org/

http://www.nelsonroadvet.com/

http://www.merckvetmanual.com/

http://avianmedicine.net/

http://www.birdsinbackyards.net/

http://Emu.tamilnadufarms.com/

http://indianfarming.in/

http://agrifarming.in/

www.ces.ncsu.edu

http://agriculture.vic.gov.au/

http://www.ajas.info/

http://www.hindawi.com/

http://smallfarm.about.com/

https://www.southernstates.com

http://www.Emufarmingindia.com/

www.agricultureinformation.com

www.countrysidenetwork.com
www.kalayaEmuestate.com
www.aea-Emu.org
www.sugarmapleEmu.com
www.abc.net.au
www.clevelandzoosociety.org
www.sybilsden.com
www.nelsonroadvet.com

Made in the USA
Coppell, TX
18 January 2020

14669301R00059